D1560005

The Next Day

Also by Melinda French Gates

The Moment of Lift

The
Next Day

*Transitions, Change,
and Moving Forward*

Melinda French Gates

FLATIRON
BOOKS
NEW YORK

www.flatironbooks.com

The credits on p. 161 constitute an extension of the copyright page.

Several paragraphs in chapter six appeared in a different form in a 2018 article by the author in *Southern Living*.

Designed by Donna Sinisgalli Noetzel

The Library of Congress Cataloging-in-Publication Data is available upon request.

ISBN 978-1-250-37865-1 (hardcover)
ISBN 978-1-250-37866-8 (ebook)

Our books may be purchased in bulk for promotional, educational, or business use. Please contact your local bookseller or the Macmillan Corporate and Premium Sales Department at 1-800-221-7945, extension 5442, or by email at MacmillanSpecialMarkets @macmillan.com.

First Edition: 2025

The text of this book is printed on a low-CO_2 intensity uncoated groundwood paper. One hundred percent of the fiber stock required to make its pages came from sawmill residuals from trees certified by the Sustainable Forest Initiative and/or the Forest Stewardship Council.

10   9   8   7   6   5   4   3   2   1

To Mom and Dad

Contents

Introduction   1

Chapter One: Find Your Small Wave   7

Chapter Two: Feel the Ease of Letting Go   25

Chapter Three: Be a Greenhouse   51

Chapter Four: Distill Your Inner Voice   77

Chapter Five: Pause in the Clearing   105

Chapter Six: Plant Roots   127

Chapter Seven: Emerge   143

Acknowledgments   155

Credits   161

. . . and there was a new voice,

which you slowly

recognized as your own,

that kept you company

as you strode deeper and deeper

into the world,

determined to do

the only thing you could do—

—Mary Oliver, "The Journey"

The Next Day

Introduction

I never expected to be writing a book like this. Then again, there's a lot that's happened in my life over the last few years that I didn't see coming.

I'm writing this at a moment of transition: a moment when one chapter has come to a close but the next has not yet begun. During this time, I've been reflecting on how we stay true to ourselves in seasons of great change and how to move forward when the ground beneath us is shifting.

You don't get to be my age without navigating all kinds of transitions. Some you anticipated and some you never expected. Some you embraced and some you resisted. Some you hoped for and some you fought as hard as you could.

Maybe you picked up this book because you are going

through a moment of transition yourself. Maybe you picked it up because someone you love is. Either way, such a time is coming. No matter who you are—man or woman, young or old—change is inevitable. The good news, though, which I have seen again and again, is that these moments of transition can be important opportunities for discovery and growth—in part because they demand often difficult, but ultimately incredibly valuable, inner work.

I've organized this book around transitions that were formative in my life. I write about leaving home for college. Becoming a parent. Losing one of my best friends to cancer. Ending my marriage. Leaving the Gates Foundation to start a new chapter in my philanthropy. Forming rituals and traditions with my family and friends. Turning sixty.

I recognize that there is much that is unique about my circumstances. I've benefited from a tremendous amount of privilege, and there's no question that has insulated me from some of life's hardships in ways that have limited my perspective.

Still, though, I believe that there are many aspects of the human experience that are universal. All of us want to feel a sense of ownership over our lives and our stories. All of us want to make meaning of the events we live through—the bitter and the sweet. All of us long for connection and the chance to be fully known.

Often when I've found myself in unfamiliar waters, I have reached across time and space to find something to buoy me in words written by someone else, sometimes someone who lived and died before I was born, someone with whom I have nothing obvious in common. In those moments, I am glad that these people took the time to write about the things that mattered to them.

One of the people whose work I have turned to is a poet named David Whyte. In the poem "What to Remember When Waking," he writes,

> *In that first*
> *hardly noticed*
> *moment*
> *in which you wake,*
> *coming back*
> *to this life*
> *from the other*
> *more secret,*
> *moveable*
> *and frighteningly*
> *honest*
> *world*
> *where everything*
> *began,*

there is a small
opening
into the day
that closes
the moment
you begin
your plans.

That poem has been on my mind a lot lately because it speaks to an important truth about transitions: The real work starts the next day. The next day—when the graduation confetti has been swept up or the wedding favors have been handed out or the movers have departed, leaving you in a sea of cardboard boxes—is when a transition truly begins. Because the next day is when we begin to make choices, sometimes unconsciously, about how we'll respond to change, what we'll carry forward and what we'll leave behind. The next day is when we start to form the next version of ourselves.

Another important truth about transitions is that they are usually easier to navigate together than alone. When you're traveling across the in-between spaces, it helps to have company. I am so honored that, by picking up this book, you have invited me to be part of your journey.

The David Whyte poem I love so much ends with a question:

What shape
waits in the seed of you
to grow and spread
its branches
against a future sky?

Is it waiting
in the fertile sea?
In the trees
beyond the house?
In the life
you can imagine
for yourself?
In the open
and lovely
white page
on the waiting desk?

As I approached my sixtieth birthday, I decided to begin filling the white pages before me with tributes to the people and ideas that have helped me through the transitions that have defined me. I like to think of others finding something in here that is helpful to them, too.

Next time you find yourself facing the unknown, I hope you'll be able to open this book to any chapter and feel a little more secure in the wake of uncertainty, a little more confident in your potential to adapt and evolve, and a little more convinced that your next day can be a place of extraordinary possibility.

Chapter One

Find Your Small Wave

As a fourth grader in Dallas, Texas, I had the chance to learn a lesson from my father that has stayed with me all my life.

The elementary school I attended at the time was run by Catholic priests and had a strict dress code with lots of rules, especially for girls. If, for example, you came in wearing a skirt the priests thought was too short, you'd be called into the office, where the principal, a nun, would take out a tape measure to check.

This day, though, the priests conducted a spot check of a different kind. They marched into my classroom and ordered all the girls to stop what we were doing and put our hands flat on the table so they could inspect our fingernails for nail polish, another dress code violation.

As I sat there with my hands splayed, I was glad that

the translucent pink polish I was wearing was so light it was almost invisible. I wasn't the kind of student who got in trouble at school, and I had no desire to be singled out.

I don't remember exactly why I happened to have nail polish on that day, but my guess, ironically enough, is that I'd put it on to look nice for church (which, in Dallas, was a real dressing-up occasion). Whatever the reason I'd polished my nails, I'm sure it never occurred to me as I did that I was breaking school rules. This was no intentional act of rebellion. Plus, it was *so* subtle that even as the priest made his rounds inspecting our hands, I was pretty sure he wasn't going to notice.

I was wrong. And, in a heartbeat, I was pulled out of my chair and dispatched to the principal's office, where I sat in a row with the other violators while the principal called our mothers (certainly *not* our fathers) to demand they come to the school with nail polish remover. Yes, right now.

I'm sure my very busy mother was annoyed to be summoned like that. There's no way she didn't roll her eyes when she got the call. She hopped in the car, though, and when she arrived at school, my two little brothers in tow, she was as pleasant as ever to the principal—even if I could tell by the squeeze she gave me that she was really on my side in the matter.

My father, on the other hand, was *incensed* when he heard what had happened. It would have been one thing if someone had noticed my nail polish and sent me home with a note saying it needed to be removed. That he would've been fine with. But he couldn't *believe* that the priest had embarrassed the girls in my class that way and then been so disrespectful of our mothers' time on top of it. He was offended both on my behalf and on behalf of my mom, who had many more important things to do that day than rush over to attend to my fingernails. So he sat me down and let me know that I shouldn't feel bad about what had happened at school—that it was the priests who were in the wrong.

I knew this wasn't something he said lightly. Both my parents were, and still are, deeply devout Catholics. They sent my siblings and me to Catholic school and took us to mass every Sunday and often during the week as well.

But as large as the church loomed in our lives, my parents were always willing to speak out against injustices they saw at our local parish, even if that meant taking on the priests. (One of their disagreements—regarding the priests' refusal to implement the reforms of Vatican II despite the parishioners' wishes—led to my mom typing up a petition and my dad collecting hundreds of signatures for it.)

I might have expected my dad to think a fuss about nail polish was some silly feminine thing he didn't need to get involved in. That's exactly why his reaction was so meaningful. He made clear to me that the way the priests treated my mother and me that day was intended to diminish us, to make us feel small and unserious, to reinforce a power hierarchy that placed us at the bottom.

But my father refused to see my mother and me that way, and in doing so, he taught me not to see myself that way either.

⁓

My dad, Ray French, is a retired aerospace engineer who worked on the Apollo project, an accomplishment that thrilled (and frankly surprised) his parents. His dad—my grandfather—owned a machine shop that just about kept the family afloat, but while his folks knew they had a brilliant son in Ray, who was already creating award-winning automotive designs in high school, they didn't have the money to send him to college. So, as family lore goes, the fall after high school, his parents put him on the train to Atlanta to attend Georgia Tech with only his paper route earnings and a jar of peanut butter to his name. Dad worked his way through college—covering his own tuition and expenses—and still managed to do well enough to earn a scholarship to Stanford, where he graduated with a master's degree in mechanical engineering.

My mom, Elaine, on the other hand, never had the opportunity to attend college. She and my dad met young and married young, and she supported him through graduate school with her job at a bottled water company before stepping out of the workforce to stay home with the four of us kids, whose daily needs she attended to largely by herself. It wasn't that my dad wasn't involved—he pitched in where and when he could—but he had a huge job and worked constantly, often sleeping on his office couch.

For all I knew, that was how every family operated. The TV shows I watched as a young girl—shows like *Little House on the Prairie* and *Leave It to Beaver*—all reinforced that model. While the men had lives and careers that took them out into the big wide world each day, the women were first and foremost mothers, expected to stay home to take care of everybody else. Most of the families I saw in real life had a similar setup. In Dallas in the seventies, I didn't know a lot of women who had careers or worked outside the home at all—unless you counted my teachers at school (many of whom were nuns!).

I'd always known that I wanted to be a mother—and that I wanted to be an excellent mother like my own. But I also wanted to be like my father, who went to work each day helping to propel giant leaps for mankind. We all took such pride in his work. One of my dad's good friends was also an Apollo engineer, and anytime there was a rocket launch, our family would all pile in the car and head to his house to watch it with his family. It was thrilling to know that two of the men sitting in the room with us had had a hand in bringing humanity to such an important moment.

I dreamed of having my own career doing something that would matter to the world and create new possibilities for the future.

That said, I just didn't have many examples of women who had both a career and family. For a while, the closest thing I had to a role model was Alexis Carrington Colby, the ruthless character on *Dynasty* whom *TV Guide* once ranked the seventh-nastiest villain in television history. Sure, Alexis was pretty despicable—but she was also one of the first depictions I saw in popular culture of a mother who also had a career outside the home that involved making decisions and controlling resources. It took a certain kind of woman to thrive in the rough-and-tumble oil industry, and even if Alexis's antics didn't always appeal to me, her ambition and drive did.

My parents had long recognized my own ambitions and were intentional about supporting them. My mother told me constantly that I could be anyone I wanted to be. "Set your own agenda or someone else will set it for you" was one of her mantras, and the answer I still give when people ask me about the best advice I've ever received.

Meanwhile, Dad helped me find a channel for those ambitions when, long before most people had personal computers at home, he purchased an Apple III computer as a gift to my sister and me and encouraged us to learn how to code. (He was aided in this endeavor by my math teacher Mrs. Bauer, who convinced our principal to buy five computers for the school and then studied computer science at night so she could teach us how to use them.) My father wanted us to believe, as he did, that my sister and I were every bit as capable of mastering this piece of cutting-edge technology as his colleagues at work.

Many years before terms like *gender equality* or *diversity* entered the corporate lexicon, my father noticed that anytime he was on a team that included a woman mathematician, that team was stronger and better for her contributions. That's why he made a special point of recruiting women to all the teams he managed. He introduced me to some of those women, which was enough for my dreams of a career in tech to start to take form.

In 2016, a wonderful movie called *Hidden Figures* told the story of three Black women at NASA who battled racism and sexism to play crucial roles in launching astronaut John Glenn, the first American in space, into his historic orbit. But back when I was growing up, stories of women like them were still mostly . . . well, hidden. Girls like me—and even more so, girls of color—didn't have a lot of female role models in science to emulate. I was lucky that my father was so intentional about introducing me to women who could help expand my sense of possibility for myself.

He did that for me in other ways, too, especially in my teenage years. Once, on a Sunday afternoon drive as a family, we passed a business park that housed a local branch of IBM. "You should tape your résumé on the door," my dad told me. "They'd be stupid not to hire you." He never missed a chance to help me see myself and my future through his eyes.

Even if he *was* my dad, it meant a lot to get a compliment like that from someone who had personally been part of something as dazzling as the Apollo missions. His faith in me gave me faith in myself. The truth is, without him, I would never have gone on to a career in computer science. In fact, I doubt I would have made it past the very first in a long series of hurdles standing between me and that career. The first major transition I ever made—leaving home and starting college—proved to be more difficult than I had expected. And when I fell into a crisis of confidence in my first semester, *his* confidence proved far more valuable than I could have possibly imagined.

Because my father's university degrees changed his life— and probably also because my mother never had the chance to pursue a degree of her own—both my parents were dead set on sending all four of their children to college. Even as busy as they were with my dad's demanding job and my mother's many responsibilities to our big family, they somehow found the energy to set up a residential real estate investment business to save up for our tuition. Money was tight during those years (there were even a few semesters when my parents went into credit card debt to cover our schooling), but they were committed to this goal and expected us to be committed to it as well.

Like a lot of girls who went to Catholic high schools, I initially assumed I would wind up at a Catholic university like Notre Dame. But in the spring of my senior year, I visited Duke University in Durham, North Carolina, and absolutely fell in love with the place. It wasn't just the beauty of the campus—it was the gleam of Duke's state-of-the-art computer lab. To me, that lab seemed like a portal into the life I wanted. It had technology that simply didn't exist on most other college campuses at the time. This, I thought, was exactly the kind of education that could set me up for the kind of career I dreamed of—one doing work that would change the world.

In August of 1982, I left Dallas, moved into an all-girls dorm on Duke's campus, and declared myself a computer science major. I was eager, excited, and (I thought) totally prepared. I'd loved high school, but by the time I reached senior year, I was ready to be done—ready to graduate, ready to leave home, ready for the next challenge to begin. I jumped into the transition with both feet and no doubts, arriving on campus with the Olympia B12 portable typewriter my parents had given me for graduation—a technological marvel, weighing in at just fifteen pounds!

(Our family had come a long way from my dad's jar of peanut butter.)

But things did not get off to an easy start. I still remember my first computer science class, taught by the head of the department. I'd met him while touring the school, and he'd seemed so nice. In the lecture hall, though, he spoke in a brusque monotone. And worse, despite the fact that I'd sailed through the computer science classes I'd taken in high school, I had no idea what he was talking about. I'd learned to program in BASIC. He was using Pascal. We literally spoke different languages.

The academic difficulties were just part of the problem. I was also experiencing culture shock. I was coming from an all-girls classroom where you raised your hand before you spoke, every single time. Suddenly, I was surrounded by these brash, arrogant guys who just shouted out the answers. I wondered how I was ever going to make my voice heard.

This was all a major adjustment for me. In high school, I'd been at the top of my class and captain of the drill team. At night, I'd gone home to a warm and loving home. Here at Duke, I was just another struggling student, and "home" was now an old dorm filled with cigarette smoke (all the other girls had taken up smoking freshman year) where everyone crowded around a TV that incessantly played soap operas.

During long, anxious nights, I would walk back and

forth between the library and the dining hall or sit at my desk listening to the unfamiliar voices bouncing off the walls of the dorm, thinking about my friends from high school who'd gone to college closer to home and wondering if I'd simply aimed too high. The first time I saw Duke's computer lab, it made me feel like anything was possible. Now, I wasn't sure if there was a place for me in it at all.

Looking back now—and having sent three kids off to college myself—I recognize that just about every college freshman has moments when they feel like a fish out of water. I didn't have that perspective yet, though. At the time, it felt like a problem that was specific to me.

If I'd packed up and gone home, transferred schools, and scrapped my plans, there is no question that my life would have been completely different. But the good news is that even at my lowest lows, I never seriously considered giving up. I still managed to trust that I was the kind of person a place like IBM would one day want to hire. And that's because my father had sent me to college with a gift more valuable than any typewriter: a belief in my own potential.

There's a parable from the spiritual teacher Ram Dass that I often think about in times of transition, one that certainly would have been helpful to me that semester.

The story begins with two waves traveling together through the ocean: one big and the other small.

As they get closer to land, the big one sees what's about to happen. One after another, the waves ahead of them are crashing into the shore—their force dissipating, their height collapsing, their imposing shape dissolving into foam. Devastated, the big wave tells the small one what is about to happen, warning in a grave voice that the end is near.

The small wave receives this warning with incredible equanimity. "Don't worry," it says. "We'll be *fine*."

"You don't understand," the tall wave insists. "This is it. We're done for."

The small wave is unmoved. "No," it says, "we're not. And I can explain why in just six words: *You're not a wave. You're water.*"

The story of the two waves is a story about possibilities. But equally as important, it's a story about the power of perspective.

As the two waves approach the shore, the tall wave can perceive what lies ahead only as a brutal ending. The small wave, though, can see the bigger picture. It understands that waves are just temporary manifestations of water's deeper, truer identity. And that understanding helps the small wave reconceptualize its collision with the shore. Instead of an ending, the collision marks a new beginning.

That's the role my father has always played for me. He is my small wave. While it took me some time to see a place for myself among the ambitious, confident young men at Duke, my dad had seen me as a future scientist or mathematician since before I'd ever stepped foot on campus. His perspective made it possible for me to power through—to remind myself that no one was born knowing Pascal and that doing big work meant doing hard work.

So I persevered. I mastered Pascal. I learned all about chips and chipsets. I joined a sorority and made some good friends. In the end, I not only finished my degree but added an MBA. All because I was lucky enough to have Dad's voice in my head reminding me of who he believed I already was and who he was confident I could become.

∿

Because my father played that small wave role for me in life, I'm always drawn to stories of other women— especially other women who work as advocates for women and girls—whose fathers played a similar role for them. Maybe that's why I have a special place in my heart for a man named Ziauddin Yousafzai.

As Ziauddin once said in a TED Talk, "In many patriarchal societies and tribal societies, fathers are usually known by their sons, but I'm one of the few fathers who is known by his daughter." His daughter, of course, being Malala, the world-famous activist for girls' education.

When Malala was a girl growing up in Pakistan's Swat Valley, the Pakistani Taliban took control of the region. Among the many other things the extremists banned— from owning a television to playing music—they declared that girls could no longer go to school. This was a heartbreaking turn of events for a curious student like Malala. But Ziauddin, who ran a girls' school in their village, refused to stop teaching. And in an incredible act of courage, Malala refused to stop learning and became an advocate for girls' education. She was only eleven years old when she started writing a blog for the BBC to let the world know what was happening in Swat Valley— and what a catastrophic waste it was to throw away the potential of girls like her.

On October 9, 2012, Malala's life changed forever. Two Taliban gunmen boarded the bus she was riding with her classmates, demanded to know which girl was Malala, and shot her in the head and neck. The Taliban wanted to silence her, but they failed spectacularly. Malala survived, and as she recovered, her crusade for girls' education not only endured; it intensified. In 2014, she became the youngest person ever to be awarded the Nobel Peace Prize.

While you likely know Malala's story, you may not know her father's. Ziauddin grew up in the Pashtun

Muslim tradition, in a remote region where marriages are usually arranged and local customs and norms place many restrictions on women's lives. Yet as a teacher and a father, Ziauddin strongly believed in treating girls equally. In a community that doesn't generally celebrate the arrival of daughters, he doted on Malala from the moment she was born, naming her after a Pashtun folk heroine, Malalai of Maiwand, a woman warrior who led Pashtun forces in battle.

In *Let Her Fly*, his book about his relationship with his daughter, Ziauddin wrote that he didn't even know what a feminist was until his family moved to the United Kingdom after the attempt on Malala's life. Still, he'd always understood that being the father of a young girl gave him a special opportunity—and a special responsibility—to be a force for change, for his daughter and others like her. "Women's voices are the most important in feminism," he later wrote in an op-ed for *Time* magazine in 2019. "But in patriarchal societies, a father's voice is perhaps the next most important tool to galvanize change."

I've gotten to know Malala through my work on gender equality. There's no question that she considers herself fortunate to have been raised by a man who saw potential in her that others could not. "It was not that my father would give long lectures or advice to me every day," Malala wrote in the foreword to *Let Her Fly*. "It was rather that his manners, his dedication to social change, his honesty, his openness, his vision, and his behavior had a big influence on me."

I love to think of all the fathers, all over the world, who have heard Malala's story and resolved to do for *their* daughters what Ziauddin did for her.

⁓

In January of 2019, my dad turned eighty. Our family came together to celebrate. The theme of the evening, in keeping with his many years of supporting the Apollo program, was "Fly Me to the Moon." Miniature astronaut figures were scattered around, and vases in the shape of the Apollo spacecraft decorated the tables.

That night, I watched my dad standing ramrod straight in his blue dress shirt as he greeted my siblings and our families at the door. Later in the evening, he scooped my mom up in his arms to take a picture—something he's been doing at family events for more than half a century. I smiled as I listened to him reflect on his life, going through each decade and calling out important moments like entering model cars into competitions in high school, attending the Seattle World's Fair, working on the design of the space shuttle and the International Space Station (still orbiting the Earth), and watching his children grow up and launch lives of their own.

When we held hands to say grace together before

dinner, we all went around and shared one thing about my dad we're thankful for. Picking just one was hard, but if I'd tried to list them all, the food would have been ice-cold by the time we started eating. I hope, though, that I've let him know in other ways how much gratitude I have for all he's done for me, from standing up for me in fourth grade, to buying that computer for my sister and me, to the ways he showed up later in my life, when things grew more complicated (like the time I was in a relationship in college that he knew I needed to get out of, and he found subtle, persistent ways to make sure I knew I deserved better).

That's why, as much as I loved the "Fly Me to the Moon" theme, it was fitting, too, that the celebration took place not in landlocked Dallas, Texas, but at a family home near San Diego—just a few miles away from the coast. While we celebrated in the house—toasting, singing, taking photos, eating good food—somewhere in the near distance, the surf pounded against the beach. One after another, the waves rolled over the sand and then receded, big waves and small waves alike, each making their own unmistakable impact upon the shore.

Chapter Two

Feel the Ease of Letting Go

I knew something was off even before I opened my eyes.

It was April 26, 1996—a Friday—around four in the morning, and my sheets were damp. Even though it had been decades since I'd wet the bed, it still took me a moment to realize what had *actually* happened: My water had broken. It was surreal. Here, at last, was the day I'd been waiting for my whole life. *I was going to become a mother.*

I tiptoed out of bed to get some towels, but I didn't make any moves to call the doctor. I didn't even wake Bill. I quietly laid a few towels down where I'd been sleeping and climbed back into bed to savor the moment. "I'm going to have a baby today," I whispered to myself. "I'm going to have a baby."

Eventually, as the first rays of sunlight began to appear,

I decided it was time to get on with things. "It's happening," I told Bill as I nudged him awake. Before calling the doctor, we shared a moment together, giggling at the bizarre and wonderful notion that, before the day was over, there would be three of us. By then, my hospital bag had been packed and ready for weeks, so after the doctor encouraged us to start making our way over, we got ourselves to the hospital pretty quickly.

The baby, however, was in no such hurry. I had been warned that with a first pregnancy, labor can last an astonishingly long time, and, as it turned out, mine was no exception. My contractions still hadn't really started yet—at least not that I could feel—and the doctor even debated sending us home to wait there instead. Ultimately, we settled on a compromise. I stayed at the hospital. Bill went to the office.

Before you roll your eyes, keep in mind that there really wasn't anything for him to do yet. Plus I had a good book with me—*The Custom of the Country* (I was on an Edith Wharton kick at the time)—so I was happy to send him off with a promise to call as soon as there were any developments.

In the end, I spent most of that magical day cheerfully alone. I walked up and down the long hallways of the Overlake Medical Center in Bellevue, Washington, immersed in Edith Wharton's story of the young beauty from the Midwest trying to crack into the high society of Gilded Age New York City. I took lap after lap, turned page after page, and silently willed the little person I was so excited to meet to please begin their descent.

It wasn't until much later that afternoon that I started active labor. Once it began, though, things got intense fast. I put down my book and dialed Bill's assistant. She had been hovering by the phone all day, waiting for this exact call—this was before we all had cell phones—and she found him right away. "You should come now," I told him in a tense voice. "You should hurry."

When he arrived, he was fascinated by everything that was unfolding. His wide-eyed wonder made me feel proud of the amazing thing my body was doing—and less self-conscious about some of the mechanics. (I did ask him to take his sweater off, though, because it smelled like the hamburger he'd eaten on the way, and I was far too nauseated to deal with that.)

They say you forget the pain of childbirth, but I haven't been that lucky. After a long, slow, almost pleasant ramp-up during the morning came hour after hour of *really* hard labor. Also, there was a complication with the baby's positioning. It was pointed in the right direction (head down) but facing the wrong way (face up). That meant that, as the baby descended, its cranium placed incredible pressure on my spine. "Back labor," they call it. I wouldn't recommend it.

For reasons that seemed obvious to me at the time—even if they're a little hard to summon or articulate now—I was determined to go through the whole delivery naturally, without any drugs. I guess I wanted the full experience, to feel every sensation. The doctor thought I was crazy, but I held out. In the end, I was in labor for fourteen and a half hours.

The hero of the day was my delivery nurse, an angel of a woman named Betsy Gruber, who let me squeeze her hand for literally hours at a time. At one point, the doctor tried to send her off to get something (and possibly to give her a break), but I wouldn't let him. "No!" I yelled, my hand clamped tight around hers. "She can't leave! She has to stay!" The doctor had to trot down the hall to get my ice chips himself.

Hour after agonizing hour, the baby descended incrementally, only to retreat again. The pressure against my spine was sickening. Toward the end, the doctor started to warn that a C-section was imminent. In a frantic effort to avoid that, I submitted to an indescribably painful attempt to draw the baby out with the help of a vacuum. I knew something was wrong when my doctor, who until then had been cool as a cucumber, suddenly started shrieking, "Turn it off! Turn it off! *Turn it off right now!*"

But then, at 6:11 in the evening, all of that faded away. Because at 6:11 p.m. on Friday, April 26, 1996, my daughter, Jennifer Katharine Gates—my Jenn—arrived into the world.

I was absolutely exhausted. I was overcome with relief. I needed a lot of stitches. But when they handed me that baby, what I was more than anything was happy, unbelievably happy.

Not everyone feels that way in the delivery room, of course, and it makes perfect sense that these bonds can take time to form. But for me, it was instantaneous. I was in love. I was absolutely smitten. I felt like I'd been hit by a truck.

I have known my whole life that I wanted to be a mother. And in the dusky hours of that spring evening, as I lay there with a damp little person all covered in vernix squirming on my chest, a new chapter began.

～◎

As anyone who has been there knows, early parenthood is a time of steep learning curves.

That's true no matter how badly you wanted to be a parent, and it's true no matter how hard you tried to prepare. For all the experience I'd had helping my mom care for my much younger brothers—and for as long as I'd been dreaming of having a child of my own—in the days and weeks after Jenn's birth, at times I felt completely incompetent as a mother.

Our last day in the hospital, I sat there staring at the little outfit I'd packed to bring Jenn home in, wondering how I was possibly going to squish those floppy little baby limbs into those tiny little arm and leg holes. I felt absolutely paralyzed. Thank God for Betsy, the gold-hearted delivery nurse. Not only did she help us get Jenn dressed, but she made a point of insisting that Bill and I take a parenting class before we were discharged. (Later, I realized that she did that to make sure Bill would know the basics and be able to help me once we were home.)

Still, when Betsy walked us out to our car and helped us maneuver Jenn into what felt like an extremely complicated little car seat and secure its very involved five-point harness, part of me wanted to ask her, "How is it possible that you're letting us go home with this baby?" She did, though. And soon, we were on our way, on the very first of what would be hundreds, maybe thousands of car rides as a family.

But first: coffee. As surreal as it felt to be driving home with a baby—our baby—in the back seat, there was a sort of normalcy to it. Enough that I decided I wanted to stop at Starbucks on the way home. In fact, I insisted on it. A skeptical Bill offered to go in and order it for me, but I was determined to do this all on my own. So he stayed in the car with Jenn while I shuffled—and, believe me, *shuffled* is a generous term to describe how I was moving at that point—across the parking lot and into the store. When I finally made it back to the car with my tall latte in hand, I felt like I'd taken an important stand. Yes, I was a mother now. But I was still *myself.*

That feeling, however, didn't last. In other moments, I was a woman I no longer recognized.

Not long after we got her home, Jenn developed a mild case of jaundice. The hospital lent us a special incubator that bathed her in therapeutic light, making her look like a tiny glowworm. We kept the incubator in her nursery, and for that first week, my wonderful mom slept in there with Jenn, waking up with her throughout the night to change her diaper and bring her into my room to nurse, which was an incredible luxury as I tried to rest and recover.

One night, Bill and I found ourselves upstairs in our room—one of the first times since Jenn was born that we'd been able to manage a quiet moment just to ourselves. I was still healing from the delivery and moving around pretty gingerly—I couldn't yet get in or out of bed in one motion—but I'd managed to get myself comfortable enough. With my mom watching Jenn downstairs, we'd propped ourselves up against the headboard next to each other and were chatting like old times.

That's when the house began to shake.

I'd been a Seattle resident for nearly a decade, but I'd

never experienced a real earthquake before—and, at 5.3 on the Richter scale, this was a *real* earthquake, its epicenter not far from our house. It took me a few beats to register what was happening—and why there was suddenly a terrible rattling coming from downstairs. Then a shot of adrenaline sent ice through my veins: *Jenn was downstairs.*

Everything after that happened very quickly. I forgot all about my stitches as I jumped out of bed and bolted for the stairs. Jenn was in the dining room with my mother, asleep in her little Moses basket in front of a shaking, rattling cabinet—the champagne glasses we'd received as a wedding gift clanging against each other, the floorboards beneath her creaking in an unnatural way. I have no memory of how I got from the bedroom to the dining room. I just remember the shocked look on Bill's face at the inhuman sounds I was making as I screamed at my mother, begging, sobbing, pleading: "Get on top of the baby! *Get on top of the baby! Mom! Mom! Get over the baby!*"

By the time I made it downstairs, the worst was already over. My mom was on her hands and knees over Jenn in her basket, looking up at me with big, kind, sympathetic eyes. I could tell that she felt sorry for me in my terror—and that even if I hadn't screamed at her like that, her own maternal instincts would have sent her flying over the baby just the same. In any case, she was safe, Jenn was safe, and the house had gone quiet.

But even so, nothing would ever be the same. My world now spun on a new axis, with Jenn at its center. I realized I would have died for her that night. I would have sacrificed Bill for her in an instant. I would have given *my own mother's* life to save Jenn's.

As much as I'd tried to prove that I was still myself—the independent woman, latte in hand—here was undeniable evidence that, at the center of my heaving chest, pulsing from my hammering heart, was a force that hadn't existed there before: a maternal love so primal and ferocious it was almost violent.

With my Jenn now back in my arms, I sank to the floor of my dining room and wept.

⁓

I share this story not because it's unique, but precisely because it isn't.

Well, okay, not every new parent comes home to an earthquake. But every parent has lived through some version of that moment, whether it's watching a child struggle for breath through one of those childhood illnesses or glancing desperately back at the car seat after a close call with a reckless driver. Whatever the threat, at some point, every parent is confronted with a simple, terrible fact: There's really only so much we can do to keep our kids safe and secure.

Which leads to an uncomfortable question.

What was all the screaming about? Who was that for? Because it wasn't for my mother—a totally competent mother of four who didn't *actually* need me to tell her what to do with a baby in an earthquake. The screaming wasn't even really for Jenn, because it ultimately didn't do anything to make her even a little bit safer.

If I'm really being honest, that screaming was for me. It was an eardrum-shattering attempt to give voice to my own deeply felt, poorly regulated, overpowering love and fear. For a moment, the intensity and chaos I was feeling on the inside spilled out into the world around me. And while I may have thought I was helping to keep Jenn safe, all I really gained from that performance was an illusion of control—and even that lasted only about a millisecond.

I'm not saying I did anything wrong. In fact, looking back, I feel a lot of compassion for that frantic thirty-one-year-old version of myself who almost ripped her stitches out lurching to protect her tiny daughter. My heart was in the right place and hammering for the right reasons.

But now I recognize that moment for what it was: a first, flailing attempt to rise to meet a fundamental challenge all parents face. We need to give our kids structure and security—without stifling their ability to learn and

grow. We need to make our presence felt and our uncon-
ditional love known—without overstepping or becoming
overbearing or pushing our children away. We need to re-
main vigilant and concerned—without allowing our own
emotions and anxieties to distract or hijack our attention.

Most of all, we need the discipline to separate our own
needs from our children's and the wisdom to know when
to let go, at least a little.

I'm lucky to have a wonderful mother. She raised my
sister, my two brothers, and me largely on her own while
my dad was working around the clock. As draining as it
must have been, she rarely showed it. She was always fully
present with us, fully engaged in whatever we were saying or doing, and absolutely steadfast in radiating warmth
and love. And she would tell you even *she* didn't get it
right all the time!

When my sister and I were teenagers, and my brothers were elementary-school-aged, my mother was working through a parenting challenge and decided to sign
up for a parenting class. She learned something there
that she later shared with me—and although I'm not
sure it's strictly backed by neuroscience, I still find it to
be instructive. Our children, they told her, come into the
world already 80 percent formed into who they are going to be. As parents, we can affect only the 10 percent
of our children's personalities on each end, helping them
to maximize their best qualities and trying to keep them

from falling prey to their worst. That means that our job as parents is to accept our children for exactly who they are and to help them nurture their strengths and manage their weaknesses—not to turn them into someone else, but so they become the best possible version of *themselves*.

That's good advice. But it's a target, not a map. Figuring out where that 80 percent ends and the part where you're desperately necessary begins? It's never totally clear. I wish I could tell you the trick for striking that delicate balance. The best I have to offer is the story of my journey toward an answer.

~

It started with what you might call an overcorrection. Consider this: The American College of Obstetricians and Gynecologists recommends that a pregnant woman gain between twenty-five and thirty-five pounds with each pregnancy. I gained seventy-nine.

To me, that weight was the external projection of something I began feeling the very second I saw the plus sign on the pregnancy test: freedom.

Freedom from perfectionism. Freedom from the crushing, relentless societal pressure to look a certain way and carefully maintain that appearance. Freedom from eating what I thought I was *supposed* to eat instead of what I really wanted. I was done with all that, I decided. Done. My body was growing a baby, and I was going to feed that body whatever it craved.

My doctor and I had some pretty contentious conversations about this at first. At every visit, I would step on the scale, and at every visit, he'd let me know exactly what he thought about how high and fast that number was rising. Eventually, I had to force a truce. Once we established that my health wasn't at risk and, more important, that the baby's wasn't either, I let him know quite forcefully that I didn't want to hear a single additional word about the topic.

So that was one way my newfound feeling of freedom manifested itself in my life. There was another, more drastic manifestation, too: I quit my job.

As I wrote in *The Moment of Lift*, I decided to leave Microsoft almost as soon as I got pregnant, and I planned my exit so that I would be retired by the time Jenn was born. My reasons were twofold. First, I already knew that I was going to *love* being a mother, and I felt very lucky to be in a position to devote myself to it full-time. Second, Bill's responsibilities at Microsoft meant that he was working many long hours and traveling a lot. I wanted to make sure this child (and any future children) would have at least one parent who aimed to be as present for them as my mother was for me.

I have a lot of happy memories from those early days. When Jenn was born, we lived just six houses down from a lake beach. Most mornings during her first few months, I'd put her in the stroller, hang all her toys on one handle, hang our lunch on another, and off we'd go down to the water, just me and my "Jenny-Jenn-Jenn." For the first time in my adult life, I didn't have a work to-do list running in the back of my mind or obligations to a team that I didn't want to let down. I was completely in control of my own time and able to spend as much of it as I wanted with my baby.

I think it's a great injustice in our society that not every new parent gets the chance to step away from work after a baby's birth. This time is essential—not only to recover from a delivery and adjust to a new routine but to bond as a family. That's a large part of why, in my work, I've become a passionate advocate for universal paid family leave for both men and women. Being able to focus on a new baby should be a right, not a privilege.

For my part, I could have lived that life forever. But inevitably, other priorities began to tug me away from the little world I'd created around Jenn and me.

The first major pull was finishing our new house, which was being built down the road. There was a lot of planning and logistics, and each step in the process always took much longer than expected. The more time I spent away from Jenn, the louder I heard an ominous voice in my head asking myself again and again in the same menacing whisper: *Are you doing enough for this baby?*

Happily, I soon had two more babies to worry about. My son, Rory, joined our family in 1999, and my daughter Phoebe followed him in 2002. In between their births, another pull on my attention emerged: Bill and I started the Bill & Melinda Gates Foundation. I hadn't planned on going back to work so soon, but suddenly there I was, feeling the need to be in meeting after meeting, doing mountains of reading to get myself up to speed on the issues, and traveling around the world to see the foundation's work in action.

In the beginning, I put strict limits around my foundation role so that I could keep my focus at home. "I am a mom first," I told my new chief of staff on his first day. "There are some boundaries around my time and my family that we are going to have to work around." I surrounded myself with people who understood that as much as I cared about the foundation's work, I also cared about doing right by my kids. I knew I was incredibly lucky to be in a position to organize my life this way. And although there were definitely times when the work crept into time I'd tried to reserve for us at home, for the most part, it worked well—or at least well enough.

But as the foundation grew, the amount of time I needed to spend there did, too. In 2005, our dear friend Warren Buffett privately let us know that he was going to transfer a significant portion of his wealth to our foundation. It was an *incredible* act of generosity, a massive gift that was going to enable us to dramatically expand our foundation's work, potentially touching millions more lives. We were, obviously, overcome with gratitude—and still are.

And yet. Jenn was nine. Rory was six. Phoebe just two. The undeniable fact was that Warren's gift would mean that their mother was going to be around a lot less, and that was a hard pill for me to swallow.

I want to be very clear that I don't think there's anything wrong with mothers spending time away from their children—not at all. There are incredible, loving mothers who have to work multiple jobs to make ends meet. There are incredible, loving mothers who choose to work because they want careers. It's a privilege to have the option to stay home with your children, and it's *also* a privilege to have the chance to do work you love. In all these regards, I was so unbelievably fortunate to have all the choices I did. But even so, I longed for a twenty-fifth hour in the day. When I look back on that chapter of my life, I remember three things: immense pride in the work we were doing at the foundation, overwhelming joy at watching my beautiful children grow up, and intense anxiety as I struggled to balance the two.

There's one day in particular I still think about—a

June day I spent in Chicago shortly after learning about Warren's gift. For Christmas that year, I'd promised Jenn a mother-daughter trip to Chicago to go to the American Girl doll store, and now it was finally here. After a special morning together picking out a doll in little-girl heaven, we were back at the hotel. Jenn was taking care of her new doll with her usual tender affection—very sweetly changing the doll's clothes and brushing her hair—as I paced a telephone cord's distance away from the desk on a call with the CEO of the foundation, Patty Stonesifer, discussing governance issues and steps we'd need to take to be responsible stewards of Warren's resources.

As we spoke, I was surprised by how hard I found myself wishing that none of this was happening—at least not now, not yet. *If only Warren could have waited ten years*, I thought to myself as I wound the telephone cord around my hand, watching Jenn play. In ten years, the kids would be teenagers. I imagined that by then, they would need so much less from me, and I would be so much more confident in my ability to do the foundation job I needed to do while also being the mother I wanted to be.

The guilt. Oh, the guilt. I felt guilty for feeling ambivalent about Warren's generosity. I felt guilty for being on the phone instead of over there with Jenn and her doll. I felt guilty that I wasn't going to be able to give the other children as much time as I'd been able to give Jenn. I felt guilty that I hadn't given Jenn more time while I still could. And then, I felt guilty for feeling guilty because the undeniable fact that I had every possible advantage a person could ever have made me even more disappointed in myself for all the ways I *still* wasn't a better mother.

What I needed to learn—but hadn't yet—was that giving into a guilt spiral like that was just another form of my scream-sobbing during the earthquake. The guilt wasn't serving anyone well. Not my children. Not my work. Not myself. It was a distraction—worse, an indulgence—that focused my attention inward instead of outward toward the people and work I loved. I was making it about *me* when it should have been about *them*.

What I needed was a new framework, one that would allow me to make peace with being less than perfect instead of obsessing over my faults and failures. Eventually, I found that framework in the concept of the "good enough" parent.

The concept traces back to a British psychologist named Donald Winnicott, who coined the phrase in the 1950s (although, in keeping with the times, he was specifically focused on the "good enough *mother*"). Even though some of his assumptions about families and gender roles are now quite outdated, the notion of a good enough parent has had notable staying power across generations of parenting experts.

Here's the central idea: A good enough parent is one who cares for their child and tends to their needs without expecting perfection of either themselves or their child. In fact, Winnicott and others argue that a good enough parent is actually *more* effective than a "perfect parent" (whatever that means) because perfectionism has no place in a healthy relationship between parent and child. A parent shouldn't waste their time and energy striving to meet some impossible standard of parenting, and they shouldn't let themselves hold their children to impossible standards either. Perfection is an unreasonable thing to expect from anyone, period.

What's more, proponents of good enough parenting believe that if a parent sets out to meet their child's every need and protect their child from every possible harm, what may appear to be selfless devotion is often, in fact, the opposite. A child whose parents are always intervening on their behalf may fail to thrive in later years when they inevitably face challenges and disappointments without their parents around to help. Under the care of a loving, good enough parent, however, a child will learn—in age-appropriate ways—how to develop inner resources and gain the tools they'll need to navigate the world on their own.

For me, the notion of the good enough parent wasn't just permission to let go. It made letting go feel essential, something I *had* to do for my children.

Of course, many parents understand this instinctively. Last spring, as part of a series of conversations I had with women about major transitions in their lives, I had the opportunity to talk about parenting with Michelle Obama, who described employing a similar philosophy with her daughters.

Michelle has lived an extraordinary life, but even with so many experiences under her belt—her law career, her work as a hospital administrator, the eight years she spent as *First Lady of the United States*—she says that when it comes to the "great learning" she's done in her life, nothing competes with raising her daughters, or, as she put it, "trying to turn those two little people into valued and valuable humans in the world." And in that project, her most important inspiration was her own mother, Marian Robinson.

"It started with her intentionally seeing us not as babies that belonged to her but as humans that she was raising up to be independent beings in the world," Michelle told me. "When you're raising people rather than babies, you make different decisions." She launched into examples. "You start thinking, okay, do I let this kid sleep with me when they're three or four because I love to cuddle with them, or do I show them that you have a bed, you can soothe yourself, you can read, and maybe you can even enjoy that time alone?" Then she put an even finer point on it: "The cuddling is for me. The sleeping in their room is to show them their independence."

What Michelle learned from her mother, she added, is that as a mother, it's not her job "to create mini-mes or people who were going to live out some brokenness in me or fill some hole or be my friend." In fact, she said with a laugh, her daughters tease her that her favorite line is "I'm not one of your little friends." But as Michelle sees it, that's just proof that she has healthy boundaries between herself and her daughters. And the ironic thing is that those boundaries, in turn, have enabled her and her daughters to have a beautiful friendship after all.

When Michelle describes what she learned from her mother (who passed away a few weeks after our conversation at the age of eighty-six), it sounds like common sense. But when I first encountered these ideas in my own motherhood journey, they felt revelatory. I had such a deep sense of guilt about leaving home to go do work in the world that it was a complete paradigm shift to consider that maybe setting that example for my children— and teaching them that the other loving adults in their lives could care for them—could be a *good* thing.

If I'm honest with myself, I knew even before I got Jenn home from the hospital that I wasn't going to be a perfect mother. But am I a good mother? I think so. And once that became the standard to measure myself against, the answer to the ever-present question "Are you doing enough for this baby?" (which later became the ever-present question "Are you doing enough for these three children?") was, in fact, yes. Of course there were a million ways I could have been a better mother. I'm sure there are also a million ways I could be a better person. But for their sake and mine, I learned to believe that while I would never be perfect, I could absolutely be *good enough.*

By releasing my grip on perfectionism and feeling the ease of letting go, I think I got a little bit closer to being the best version of a mother I can be.

In February 2023, on one of those gray and windy winter days in New York City, Jenn and I were back in labor and delivery together. But this time, she was the one bringing a daughter into the world. In one of the greatest gifts anyone has ever given me, she and her wonderful husband, Nayel, invited me to be part of that special day.

Among the many other things I felt as I watched Jenn prepare to give birth, I was blown away by her calm and competence. Anyone who saw Jenn playing with her new doll that day in Chicago could have guessed she'd make a great mother. Since then, she's earned a degree in biology from Stanford, a master's of public health from Columbia, and a medical degree from Mount Sinai. She was as prepared to step into this role as anyone could possibly be.

At one point during our long day together, she told Nayel and me that we'd need to leave the room. We looked at each other and stammered that of course we would. We figured she wanted some privacy and said she should just let us know as soon as she wanted us to come back. She laughed at us. "No, no," she explained. "It just needs to be sterile for me to get my epidural."

As the night wore on, I stepped away so that she and Nayel could be together as a couple for the beautiful birth that followed. The next morning, I woke up to an early-morning call from my younger daughter, Phoebe, who had hounded Nayel for updates from the delivery room until she became the first to know. "The baby came!!" she squealed through the phone, the most excited new aunt you've ever heard. I got ready as fast as I could and headed to the hospital, driving along the Hudson River under the wet gray sky. When I got back to their room, Jenn and Nayel introduced me to my first grandchild. Her name is Leila, which means *night* in Arabic. Leila Grace.

As Jenn and Nayel rested after a long, intense night, I sat on a small sofa in their hospital room, holding little tiny Leila against my chest. I sat there like that for hours, long enough to watch the sun break through the clouds and light up the sky with pinks and reds, until it finally sank down somewhere back beyond the bridge. Jenn slept fitfully through the early evening, frequently slipping out of bed to check on her newborn daughter. "I just want to see her," she told me. We both gazed at this miraculous little creature until, secure in the knowledge that her baby was okay, Jenn was ready to go back to try to rest some more.

With my daughter sleeping in her bed, and her daughter sleeping on my chest, all of us warm and cozy inside as a glorious winter sunset marked the end of Leila's first day on earth, I felt my heart spilling over with love and tenderness for them both. I knew that even as she slept, Jenn's world was changing. That she would wake up the next day to find herself at the beginning of her own journey as a parent, one that would ignite her own raging maternal love, one that would test her strengths and limits, one that would teach her how terrifying it is to love someone as deeply as I love her and Rory and Phoebe— and one that I hoped would lead her to a place as happy and at peace as I felt that day.

Whatever this journey brings you, Jenn, I hope you will always remember, my love—for your sake and your children's—that exactly who you are is exactly what they need, and that even more important than giving them everything is trusting yourself to know that you are already enough. So much more than enough.

And to any other parent who is reading this, know that

this is every bit as true for you. When it comes to taking care of your family—some of the most important work you'll do in this world—I hope you'll refuse to let perfectionism rob family life of precious joy. Allow yourself, too, to feel the ease of letting go.

Chapter Three

Be a Greenhouse

The first time I picked up the phone to call John Neilson, I had no idea I was making the first overture in what would eventually develop into one of the most meaningful friendships of my life. Frankly, I just needed a ride.

It was the spring of 1987, shortly after I'd accepted a job at Microsoft. I was still finishing up my MBA at Duke, but that week, all ten members of my hiring class were in Seattle for orientation. I'd flown across the country, rented a car, and driven out to the Microsoft campus in Redmond, Washington, where we'd spent a long day sitting in the boardroom, listening to an assortment of vice presidents and division managers.

It was a testosterone-laden affair—I was the only woman in my hiring class—but I noticed right away that a couple of the guys seemed really friendly, especially a tall, lanky redhead at the other end of the conference table who went out of his way to make everyone feel comfortable.

Later that day, after our meetings were over, I went apartment hunting, which was going fine until I ran over a curb and popped a tire on the rental car. There I was, sitting by the side of the road in a strange city, trying to figure out a course of action. *The tall redhead*, I thought. *He was nice. Probably my best bet. What's his name again? John...John Neilson.* I fished out my keycard with the number for the Residence Inn where we were all staying, wandered around the neighborhood until I found a pay phone, and made my first call to my future colleague— who was soon to become one of my best friends.

John, being John, immediately agreed to drive out to pick me up. As he would go on to prove again and again, he was always someone you could count on in a pinch. We fell easily into a long conversation. He was so excited to tell me about his fiancée, Emmy. He was a fast talker, and he had a lot to say about her: how they'd met in high school, how curious she was, how fun she was, how much he was looking forward to being married to her.

A few months later, the proud recipient of a brand-new MBA, I was back in Seattle with my mom to move into my new apartment. While I waited to get the keys, we were once again staying at the Residence Inn where Microsoft always put up its guests. One night as we were getting back from our errands, we bumped into John, who was on his way out, hand in hand with a young woman. "John!" I shouted across the lobby, excited to see a friendly face. We hugged. "And you must be the famous Emmy."

Even though we'd only spent a short time together, he'd left a big impression, so I was happy to see him and introduce him to my mom. After we'd gone our separate ways, my mom articulated my thoughts exactly when she turned to me and said, "Well, they seem *terrific*." I felt like I had already made my first friend at my new job.

The next time I saw John, we were both officially working at Microsoft, and he and Emmy were officially married. He was already on his way to establishing his reputation as a popular and accomplished executive, famous for his work ethic and his sense of humor and the fact that he seemed to own a grand total of three dress shirts (*all* of them wrinkled, *all* of the time).

People absolutely loved working for him. As one guy on his team described it to me, "John had an almost supernatural belief in what we were doing as a company and the charisma to help you see his vision."

There were so many examples of why our colleagues adored him, but here's one of my favorites: Once, John had his eye on a talented young man he wanted to recruit to Microsoft. The only problem was that the young man had absolutely no intention of working there. He had already basically accepted an offer from another company, which had extended him a plum deal and the chance to live and work in Malaysia. When John insisted on flying him out to Seattle to talk about a job, the recruit said yes to be polite—but his first stop was at Nordstrom to buy tropical shirts for Kuala Lumpur.

You can probably guess how this story ends. It only took John one day and a "dude, you've got to change your flight" (it was always "dude" with John) to change the guy's mind. Even decades later, he remembered being absolutely blown away by John's vision, John's passion, John's humor—and the fact that John had invited him to his house for a homemade dinner with Emmy. That really caught his attention. "For all of the passion and purpose John brought to his work," the man later told me, "he also had a lot of empathy and humanity." As John proved the day he drove out to rescue me—a near stranger—in addition to being uncommonly brilliant and uncommonly motivated, he was also uncommonly kind.

Even though John and I both got our start at Microsoft in product marketing, we didn't really get close until we were sent on a business trip—I can't remember if it was to Chicago or New York. One of John's defining features, I quickly came to learn, was his sense of adventure. At one point during the trip, John mentioned that he'd always wanted to go skydiving. I was immediately intrigued. "I would *totally* do that," I told him. Then we cooked up the idea to convince Emmy and Bill to join us. (John was one of the very few people at work who knew I'd recently started dating Bill.)

On a bright weekend morning not long afterward, the four of us met up at Bill's house to drive the forty-five minutes to the jump site in Snohomish, all jitters and butterflies. Even as she got in the car, Emmy seemed certain we wouldn't follow through. But as much as each of us probably considered backing out for a moment or two (well, maybe not John), no one wanted to be the one to chicken out. Somehow, we each held it together long enough for all four of us to make the jump. There's a picture of us that hung on my wall for years, taken shortly after we landed, our arms around each other, giggling with joy and adrenaline.

That day in Snohomish, on a bumpy plane roughly three thousand feet above ground, the seeds of a very deep friendship began to form. In fact, I'm not even sure *friendship* is a big enough word for it. I once told John that next to our children and families, Bill and I considered our relationship with John and Emmy to be one of the most important things in our life. The four of us came together right at the threshold of adulthood, and in a way, we grew up together. In *Crossing to Safety*, a novel the four of us read together about a similarly deep friendship between two couples, the author Wallace Stegner describes their friendship as "a relationship that has no formal shape, there are no rules or obligations or bonds as in marriage or the family, it is held together by neither law nor property nor blood, there is no glue in it but mutual liking. It is therefore rare."

Rare is a good word for it. Rare and precious.

Over the course of the next decade, there were many more adventures together as a foursome, many laughs, so much joy. There was, for example, the rainy weekend we decided to drive down the coast of Oregon to a lodge we'd heard about. Only after we started driving did we realize that, somehow, none of us had stopped to calculate how long it would take to get there. (John and I were always the organizers of the adventures, so I'll admit that was probably on us.) The journey turned out to be much, much longer than we'd imagined, and we ended up spending most of the weekend in the car. But with John and Emmy, even *the drive* was fun. When we finally made it to the lodge, we took beach walks and stayed up late watching movies, but honestly, the best part of the trip was the time we spent crammed into the car, listening to John and Emmy take turns reading Henry James's *The Turn of the Screw*. That's a special kind of friendship.

Another time, the four of us went to see *Cyrano de Bergerac* as part of a theater festival. After the final climactic scene where Cyrano dies moments after his beloved Roxane finally tells him she loves him too, all four of us were crying so hard that we had to stay in our seats long after everyone else had left. "A well-done love story," was all I could choke out as we finally gathered ourselves together enough to make a very sniffly exit.

This all took place against a backdrop of endless puzzle nights, Scrabble battles, and games of doubles tennis. Once—and to be honest, we're lucky it happened even once—Emmy and I beat Bill and John in doubles(!), and as our reward, the men had to cook us a lavish seafood dinner. Bill kept insisting he'd made the clearly store-bought hollandaise sauce himself, but no one believed him for a second.

John and Emmy also played a big role in helping Bill and me navigate the early years of our relationship. We were one of those on-again, off-again couples, and both of us leaned on John and Emmy during the ups and downs. I later told John, "Only you two know how much you helped in getting us to the point of marriage." We invited them to join us on the engagement trip we took to East Africa—my first trip to the continent and the one where Bill and I decided together that we would use the money from Microsoft to focus on the world's poorest people. It was a turning point in my life, and I am so glad that John and Emmy were part of it, emerging from their tent each morning in canvas hats and matching khakis and great big grins. (Emmy, it turned out, developed an enthusiasm for bird-watching that trip—*not* something we would have anticipated.) When we got married in Hawaii on New Year's Day 1994, they were standing with us in our wedding party as we made our vows.

Part of the reason our friendship got so deep so fast, I think, is that it came at such a special moment in our lives. It began before we had kids, before the pressures of work became too intense, before Bill was really in the spotlight. From the first time we were all together that day in Sno-homish, I think all four of us felt like we were at the very beginning of something special. We were so excited to have found each other and for all that we wanted to do to-gether. We thought this was the prelude. It never occurred to us that it might be the final act.

But then, in December 1997, came the phone call that changed everything.

I wish I could tell you where I was or what I was doing when the phone rang at our home outside Seattle that day. But the truth is, it was a pretty unremarkable day, and getting a phone call from John wasn't anything unusual. We'd talked on the phone many, many times since that long-ago day I'd called him to ask for a ride.

But as soon as I heard his voice, I could tell this wasn't an ordinary call. "Melinda," he said, his tone almost apol-ogetic. "They found a tumor in my chest."

I knew that John had been sick before. As a teenager,

he had lived through testicular cancer. Years later, he and Emmy used IVF to conceive their three children using sperm he'd frozen before his treatments began. But we all thought that horrible chapter was behind him.

This time, he told me, it was non-Hodgkin's lymphoma, and it was advanced. It was clear to everyone—to his doctors, to John and Emmy, and now to me—that this was a dire situation. I kept it together on the phone, and so did he. He told me he was determined to beat it, and I promised to help in any way I could. It didn't feel like the beginning of a goodbye.

But I woke up the next day to that deeply unsettled feeling you get the morning after something terrible has happened. My body remembered something was wrong before my mind was awake enough to remember what. *Something changed yesterday*, a voice whispered as I tunneled my way out of sleep. And then the jolt. *Oh my God. John.*

That day, and for many days that followed, I was absolutely overcome by sadness. I was sad for John and all that he was so courageously preparing himself to endure. I was sad for Emmy, who I knew had to be *terrified*—not to mention overwhelmed by taking care of three young children while also being there for her seriously ill husband. And my heart ached for their children, too. They were about to confront a lot of very difficult things that no one their age should have to.

Underneath all the sadness, I also felt helpless. My two dear friends were stepping into the unimaginable, and I had no idea how to accompany them through it. I'd never known anyone who was sick before. The only people I'd lost in my life were grandparents. I didn't know what being a good friend to John and Emmy through this would look like. I wasn't even sure where to begin.

Growing up Catholic, at school and in church, I had learned the famous prayer of Saint Francis of Assisi, the one that begins, "Lord, make me an instrument of your peace." There is a line toward the end where Saint Francis asks God to "grant that I may not so much seek to be consoled as to console." That prayer was on my mind often in those days as I tried to figure out my role in what was about to unfold. I desperately wanted to be a source of consolation for John and Emmy. And I promised myself that I wouldn't let the fear of saying or doing the wrong thing create a wedge between me and them. Even though I wasn't going to get it right all the time, I was going to try everything I could.

⁓

There's a practice called Ring Theory, developed by a psychologist named Susan Silk, that offers guidance for helping someone you care about navigate a crisis. While I didn't learn about it until many years after John's illness, I've found it to be a valuable framework when people you love are going through something difficult.

In Ring Theory, you write down the name of the person experiencing the crisis and draw a circle around it. In this case, the name in the center of the circle would have been John's.

Around that circle, you draw a slightly larger circle to represent that person's immediate family—in this case, Emmy and the kids. Around that circle, you draw another slightly larger one to represent their close friends. (That's where I would have put myself.) The concentric circles keep expanding—one for more casual friends and more distant family members, another for professional acquaintances, and so on.

Once you have your circles all sorted out, you follow one simple rule: "comfort in, dump out." The person at the center of the circle is encouraged to ask any favor, make any request, complain whenever they feel like it, and be extended any grace by anyone in any of the circles around them.

His immediate family is allowed to do those things, too, but not to him—only to the people outside their circle.

And as far as friends like me, I could cry to Bill, complain about the horrible senseless loss to any of my other friends, or vent about my anger and frustration to my parents or siblings—but I absolutely could not direct any of that toward John or Emmy or anyone else closer to the crisis than I was. Even when it was difficult, I had to remember that it wasn't my place to call Emmy asking for updates or to ever let John know that I wished I was being given more chances to spend time with him. My role was to do everything I could to lift John and Emmy up and to avoid absolutely anything that risked dragging them down. I could *console* but never *seek to be consoled.*

There were definitely times when that required an uncomfortable amount of restraint. When John and Emmy were right in the thick of things, they didn't always have time to stay in close touch—and I had to learn to accept that no matter how much of my day I spent thinking about them and wondering how they were doing, I would have to wait for them to update me at a moment that was right for them. I desperately wanted to spring into helpful action, but there were a lot of instances when the most important thing I could do was just make sure they knew I was waiting in the wings if they needed me.

Later that year, there was a moment when things looked hopeful. John underwent radiation treatment at the University of Washington, and at first, it was a success. He started planning to return to work at Microsoft. But in the fall, the cancer came back. The tumors began to spread rapidly. And John's doctors in Seattle found themselves at a loss.

John and Emmy weren't ready to give up. Emmy's mother came to take care of the kids, and John and Emmy temporarily relocated to Illinois for a series of experimental treatments at the University of Chicago. John was going through hell, and Emmy wanted to make sure he wasn't alone for it.

For all the times I felt helpless during that season, one weekend I had an idea that I thought might actually work. I was quite pregnant at the time but still able to travel, so I called Emmy and offered to switch places. "I know how much you miss the kids," I told her. "If you want to come home to see them for a few days, I'll go stay with John. I'll sit by his bedside in silence if that's what he most needs." I could tell that Emmy was torn— anyone would be—between being there for John and being there for her kids. Ultimately, she decided to take me up on it. I packed up and boarded a flight to Chicago. When I got off, Emmy stepped onto the same plane to fly back to Seattle.

I was already in my third trimester, so my footsteps were heavy as I walked down the long hallway to John's room, bracing myself for what I was about to see. I tried to prepare for the sight of my tall, redheaded, vibrant, crinkly-eyed friend ravaged by disease. I took a deep breath and gently opened the door.

I wish I could say that I felt nothing but relief at seeing him—but the truth is that it was every bit as hard as

I'd imagined. He was a specter of his former self. Always lanky, now he was emaciated. He lay in the hospital bed with a hat on his bald head and the covers up to his chin because he was freezing. I don't know if you've ever seen someone you love suffering from advanced cancer, but I hope you never have to.

John was so desperate to live for Emmy and the kids, but he knew the odds weren't good, and, after so many painful treatments, he was simply exhausted. The change wasn't just physical. John had never been religious, but in the last few months of his life he became extremely spiritual. We talked about that while I sat on the sofa in his hospital room. And then he peered out from over the bedsheets, cleared his throat, and looked me in the eyes.

"There's something I want to tell you," he began, his voice uncharacteristically slow and quiet. "Something I need you to do for me."

"Of course," I told him. "Anything, John, anything." I had been waiting for so long to be told how I could help.

"It's about Emmy," he said. I leaned in closer to make sure I could hear every word. "She deserves, Melinda, to have another best friend in life. We've been best friends. We've known each other since high school. She deserves to have another best friend. And I want you to remind her of that."

I thought I knew what he was getting at, and then he made it even clearer. "So if she gets to the point, Melinda, where she questions if she should marry somebody again,

I want you to remind her that I thought that that would be a good path for her to choose."

That was John—always thinking of others, even in the face of death. I felt like he implanted some small part of himself within me—his selflessness, his enormous capacity to love—in that moment, and I wanted to live up to what he had asked of me. Yes, I promised him. I would be there to help Emmy find love again.

Eventually, he got tired and told me it was okay to go back to my hotel now. Before I shut the door behind me, my eyes lingered on my friend, contemplating all that fierce love and loyalty blazing beneath his thin and pale skin.

One of my favorite writers, Mark Nepo, has a poem called "The Work of Care." It begins, "I'm not sure I can help / but my heart wants to try" and builds toward the most soaring ending.

> *But when the hunger is*
> *inside, when the break is*
> *where no one can see,*
>
> *then all we can do is*
> *be a greenhouse for*
> *each other.*

"Be a greenhouse for each other." I've always found that turn of phrase so beautiful, that aspiration so generous and wise. Maybe, the poem suggests, the most important thing we can do for a friend is to cultivate a place within us where the things they plant can grow. As John's friend, I could carry forward some of his selflessness and enormous capacity for love. As Emmy's, I could carry forward her unbelievable courage and indescribable grace. Even just the thought made me feel closer to them.

After it became clear that John wasn't going to get better, he spent his last few months journaling his values for his kids and making arrangements—for Emmy and the kids, mostly, but also for his own memorial (which he insisted on calling his "wedding" so it wouldn't sound so sad). During those weeks, I didn't hear from them much.

But I took advantage of that time to do something I'd been putting off for way too long: I wrote John a letter. I'd started and stopped so many times, feeling like nothing I could put down on the page was worthy of my friend, who was a huge literary buff and a beautiful writer himself. But reading *Crossing to Safety*, the novel about the friendship between couples, had always made me want to write down the details of our friendship for posterity.

"When I think back on our friendship," I wrote, "the first thing that comes to mind is any one of us—and often all four of us—with our heads thrown back in sheer, belly-rolling laughter." Over the years, we had given each other an incredible gift—"the freedom to have fun." And

I wrote for eleven pages about all the adventures we'd been on together, all the fun we'd had.

"It will be so hard for us to say goodbye. We are already struggling with it," I wrote in the last paragraph. And then I made a point of making sure he knew that I was going to honor his request. "We will be here for Emmy in any way she needs us," I promised him. "We love you, John. I love you."

Not long after that, I got a call from Emmy. John had stopped all treatment and entered hospice care. And although Emmy didn't say it in as many words, her message was clear: The end was near.

The days that followed were restless and eerie. I was more than nine months pregnant. Any day now, my son would be entering the world. Any day now, my best friend would be leaving it. There was anticipation and dread, joy and grief. Also, a sense of the surreal, something otherworldly. I was suspended at the very edges of life.

As desperate as I was to see John and be a loving presence for him through all that was happening, I tried to maintain a respectful distance so that he could spend his final days with his full attention on Emmy and the kids. Emmy and John were so thoughtful about how they folded their children into this experience—how they found age-appropriate ways to ensure that his death wasn't some abstract, scary thing to them. In those last days, I'm told, the kids were in and out of his room often and could be heard from John's bed, playing happily downstairs with Emmy's mom.

When Emmy felt like calling, I dropped everything to spend as much time on the phone as she needed, murmuring words of comfort and carving out a safe and supportive place for her to process the experience out loud—trying to make myself a greenhouse, holding her in warmth and light. And so she wouldn't have to keep repeating the same updates over and over again, I passed along anything she wanted people to know to the next ring of people around us.

"She says John is super at peace," I emailed our friend Tricia after one of those calls. "He told the hospice yesterday that this was emotionally the hardest thing he has ever done yet, but he is not ready to go because it's the most fun time he has ever had with Emmy. Isn't that amazing?" I signed off with an update on the baby. "If labor doesn't kick in these next 48 hrs, doctor will move things along this weekend," I wrote. "I am super ready."

Once it became clear that the baby had no intention of budging on his own, Bill and I prepared to go to the hospital to begin an induction. Before that, though, we asked Emmy if it would be okay if we came over. We didn't know how long I'd be in the hospital once I started to deliver or if John would still be with us when I got out. I didn't want to miss my chance to say goodbye.

By then, John didn't have the energy for long visits, so our conversation was short but wrenching. He told me he was having trouble breathing. I repeated what I'd told him in the letter about how much he meant to me. I told him how much I loved him. I told him that I would be giving his name to my son. As I sank back into the car, my cheeks wet with tears, the seat belt cutting into the hard round drum of my belly, it occurred to me that John might die that very night.

He didn't, though. Or the next day either. In fact, the last photo I have with John was taken on his front porch a few days later, when I stopped at his house on my way home from the hospital. Emmy's camera captured me looking exactly how most women look just days after giving birth—puffy and robust, swollen and vibrant, proud and exhausted. John is gaunt, clearly in the last days of his life, his handsome face reconfigured into what his doctor later described as "the pallor of death."

But there is joy in that picture, too, because on his lap, he's holding my son, Rory Gates. Rory *John* Gates.

~~

When the end did come, it was a Saturday. Emmy had stayed up with John through a long and difficult night, holding his hand and timing her long, smooth breaths with his ragged ones. Eventually, the sun came up. The sounds of their children playing started filtering in. And that's when my incredible friend Emmy—braver than I ever knew anyone could be—whispered the kindest words she could have said:

"John, you can go. It's okay. I'm going to be okay."

And he left.

⁓

"Grief," wrote the psychologist Mary-Frances O'Connor, "is the cost of loving someone." She wasn't just waxing poetic; she was making a scientific observation.

Loving someone, she explained in an interview with *Scientific American*, "updates the physical connections between neurons, and it changes the way that proteins are folded" in our brains. In simpler terms, "it changes the wiring."

When we lose someone we love, our brains struggle to adjust to their absence. Love is what psychologists call a "bonded relationship"—it relies on our belief that we and the people we love will always be there for each other. And when that's no longer true, at least in a physical sense, it can feel like part of you is missing. In fact, O'Connor argues, a part of you *is* missing. "The absence of that person," she says, "is like an amputation."

"Grieving," she continues, "can be thought of as a form of learning." Our brains eventually do the work of adapting to our new reality. And at least one study suggests that, perhaps because our brains are doing that work, we may even experience some positive growth in the bargain, in the form of more "meaningful interpersonal relationships" or "an increased sense of personal strength."

I can't tell you I felt much of anything positive in the weeks and months after John died, but I do connect with the idea that grief is more than simply looking back at what we've lost—it's something that propels us forward into a new understanding of who we are and the person we loved.

So, when I think about the story of losing my friend all these years later, I'm able to feel relief that, while his last few months were painful, they were also peaceful. I'm able to take some solace in the fact that he had the opportunity to say goodbye to the people in his life. And I'm able to be grateful that, as a final gift, he gave us something else to do for him after he was gone: Before he died, he asked Bill and me if we would host his memorial service in our backyard. Because he wasn't religious, he didn't feel right about the ceremony being in a church— nor did he want it to be in some anonymous banquet hall or dining room. He wanted it to be in a place that felt warm and familiar. Of course we said yes.

In the first days after his death, it was helpful to have tasks. We plowed our grief into preparations for John's "wedding." We ordered food, got a tent set up, worked on our remarks, and ultimately lucked into a mild and beautiful spring day.

It meant a lot to be able to do something for John and Emmy. But I was grateful the funeral was at our house for another, more practical reason, too: I had an eleven-day-old baby who was still nursing so often we couldn't be apart yet. So the morning of the service, I got myself dressed in whatever I could find that fit, and Bill, Rory, and I headed downstairs together to join the others who had gathered to celebrate John's life.

When it was our turn to speak, Bill and I joked about John's extensive vocabulary—he'd told Emmy that one of her ideas for the memorial was "too pedantic"—and I read a bit of poetry by Percy Bysshe Shelley, one of John's favorites:

> *He is made one with Nature: there is heard*
> *His voice in all her music, from the moan*
> *Of thunder, to the song of night's sweet bird;*
> *He is a presence to be felt and known*
> *In darkness and in light, from herb and stone,*
> *Spreading itself where'er that Power may move*
> *Which has withdrawn His being to its own;*
> *Which wields the world with never-wearied love,*
> *Sustains it from beneath, and kindles it above.*

Then Emmy talked about how John had asked her to speak on the topic of love.

"Could you narrow that down a bit?" she'd asked him.

"No," he'd said.

"Well, then," she'd replied, "who would you suggest to be my backup if I can't pull it off?"

She did, though, and beautifully, talking about how she would "concentrate on a little bud" inside of her. "This bud is you," she told John. "All that I know John Neilson was, is inside this bud. And I will water it daily until some day long from now, it blooms so big and so beautiful that it fills this empty hole." *All we can do is be a greenhouse for each other.*

After Emmy finished, other friends and family members took turns standing up and sharing favorite memories of John. It was a wonderful, very personal service—the perfect celebration of our friend. I spent most of it in a chair in the shade, nursing Rory under a blanket draped over my shoulder, exchanging memories of John with the steady stream of people who stopped to say hello.

It's hard to describe how profound the experience was—what it felt like to sit there at the edge of the water under that bright blue sky, grappling with an almost incomprehensible ending, while at the same time holding in my arms the physical embodiment of a new beginning, his tiny mouth making sweet smacking sounds against my breast.

There, that afternoon, in a flow of tears and milk, I felt part of something much bigger than myself. Part of a force that binds us all, a circle of life that connects and

completes. I thought again of Saint Francis of Assisi. "For
it is in giving that we receive," he says. "It is in pardoning
that we are pardoned. And it is in dying that we are born
to eternal life."

~

The next day is when the healing began. In the weeks
and months that followed, I spent a lot of time with
Emmy, doing my best to help carry her across her grief
(just as, after my divorce years later, she would carry me
across mine). Eventually, she did find a new best friend,
marrying a man who, fittingly enough, she'd originally
met through John. Her three children grew up to be wonderful people who each remind me of John in different
ways.

I'll always be grateful to John for the way he managed
to plant himself inside each of us, making sure we'd be
there for each other even after he was gone, allowing us the
chance to be that greenhouse so beautifully described in
the poem I love so much. And, of course, as Emmy predicted, the little bud John planted in the people who loved
him continued to blossom and grow.

In 2011, I took a trip to a meditation center in the
Hudson River Valley. On my first day there, I was walking along an outdoor path to my room, birds chirping
overhead, when a woman hurried up beside me with an

urgent look on her face. "You said you were at Microsoft," she said. "What years were you there?" I wasn't sure where she was going with this, but I told her. I was anticipating some question about Bill, but she took the conversation in a totally different direction. "I'm wondering," she asked me, "if you ever knew a man named John Neilson."

Even just hearing his name made me startle. Yes, I told her. I knew John. More than that, I said, I loved John. He was one of the best friends I've ever had.

"Oh my God," the woman gasped. "I worked under him in the sales office in New York. He was one of the most meaningful people I've ever met in my whole life."

Me too, I told her. Me too.

And suddenly, for a moment—more than a decade after John's spirit slipped out of the sunlit bedroom ringing with his children's voices, his hand still clasped between Emmy's—he was back. He was right there between us. As the woman and I started trading happy memories of our friend, I realized he was once again doing what he always did: bringing people comfort, making them feel special, making them smile.

For so many years, I have missed John so, so much, but that day, for a moment, I didn't have to.

Chapter Four

Distill Your Inner Voice

It was the end of 2019, and I'd been having the same nightmare for weeks.

In the beginning, I'd be standing in a house, a beautiful house. Then I'd realize that it was falling apart, its foundation hollowed out, eroded away by the ocean. The floor beneath me would start caving in. Night after night, I woke up panicked. I'd lie there heaving, reminding myself to take deep breaths.

I didn't need Sigmund Freud to tell me what these dreams were really about. If anything, the metaphor was a bit obvious. Bill has publicly acknowledged that he wasn't always faithful to me while we were married. That October, things had reached a fever pitch when *The New York Times* published a deeply disturbing article that raised serious questions about Bill's conduct—questions that suggested he had betrayed not only our marriage but also my values.

There had been other difficult periods in our relationship, other moments when it felt like things could have fallen apart. But we loved each other, and we loved the family we'd built together, so every time cracks appeared in our union, we'd found ways to patch them up. Besides, I was raised Catholic, in a family that took marriage very seriously and meant it when we said "'til death do us part." I had worked hard to make our marriage work because the idea of leaving had always felt almost unimaginable.

And yet, in those last weeks of the year, the nightmares seemed to be signaling something to me. After so many nights dreaming about crumbling foundations, one night my subconscious offered up a different vision. I dreamed we were all standing on a cliff—me, Bill, the kids—when the ledge I was standing on cracked off, and I plummeted away from my family. Even after my eyes flashed open, the fear and loneliness lingered. As dramatic as it sounds, I knew, in that moment, that I was going to have to make a decision—and that I was going to have to make it by myself.

Soon after, I started to hear a whisper at the edge of my consciousness, the barest echo of a voice. It spoke with gentle authority, softly sharing its sad and solemn message: *This isn't right anymore.*

That was, to be honest, a terrifying thing to contemplate. And so at first, I tried to push the whisper away. I distracted myself with a long work trip and a visit to my daughter Phoebe, who was doing a semester abroad in South Africa. I threw myself into the winter holidays. At the end of the holidays, I called my best friend from high school, Mary Lehman, and begged her to get on a plane. I didn't want to be alone with my thoughts. I needed to talk.

Trying to ignore the whisper hadn't worked. It just grew louder and more insistent. It wasn't unkind. It wasn't demanding. It was just . . . *there*, all the time, repeating the same message over and over.

Finally, at the end of my wits, I decided that if I couldn't turn away from the voice, I would fully turn toward it instead. By then it was a new year, 2020. I planned a trip to New Mexico, intending to spend the last days of February alone, reflecting and journaling—an impromptu silent retreat of sorts. At the last minute, though, I invited Bill to come with me. I was so committed to trying to save our marriage that I didn't want to pass up a chance for us to break out of our routine and do something as a couple. I thought being together in a new context might help us. He said yes, and we flew together to Santa Fe.

When we arrived at the rental house, I settled in and started exploring, opening doors and peeking into closets, checking out the views from different windows. The house was furnished, and there were photographs throughout of the family who owned it. As I followed their faces from room to room, piecing together their story, I realized something eerie: The only reason the house had been available for us to rent was that the couple—the couple who had lived a life together between these walls—had split up. I typed their names into my phone and looked them up. He'd already remarried. I wondered where his former wife was and how she was doing. I hoped she was okay.

At first, Bill and I tried to treat it like any other vacation. We hiked. We had dinner together. But I also made sure to intentionally set aside time for the quiet reflection I had originally planned on doing. And one night, while I was sitting downstairs by myself with a pen and my journal, I realized with a start that I knew why I'd come to New Mexico.

My inner voice began to speak again, and this time its words were firm and conclusive: *It's time to separate yourself from Bill.*

~⊃

Many years ago, I discovered the work of Jon Kabat-Zinn, a mindfulness teacher and prominent professor of medicine.

I was drawn to how he described the various levels of

human consciousness. In his bestselling book *Wherever You Go, There You Are*, Kabat-Zinn explains, "From the Buddhist perspective, our ordinary waking consciousness is seen as severely suboptimal, both limited and limiting, resembling in many respects an extended dream rather than wakefulness." The work he does in this area is about teaching people to pierce our ordinary waking consciousness—the suboptimal state in which most of us travel through the world—in order to access "the full spectrum of our conscious and unconscious possibilities."

We all approach mindfulness in our own way. But however we get there, the relationship we have with ourselves—with the true, authentic selves that live beneath our ordinary waking consciousness—is, I've learned, one of the most important relationships we'll ever have.

My own relationship with my deeper self began in high school. It was one of many gifts I received from the liberal order of Ursuline nuns who ran the all-girls high school I attended. The sisters fashioned a "chapel" for us out of two adjoining classrooms and encouraged us to spend a lot of time in there, learning to adjust to the quiet and stillness, opening ourselves up to what lies within us. That makeshift chapel is where I first started learning to hear my own inner voice.

If I could go back in time, I would tell my younger self—that restless young woman fidgeting in her pressed white blouse and plaid uniform skirt—how lucky she was to be learning those lessons as a teenager, to be working so early in life to develop the discipline to distill the inner voice inside her. From the vantage point I have now, I'm honestly quite impressed with how well I knew myself as a high school student. As young as I was, I emerged from those quiet sessions in the chapel with a strong sense of who I was and what was important to me. That has given me a home base to return to, over and over again, helping me to set the course of my life and correct my bearings when I get lost.

When I left Ursuline Academy for college, and then college for Microsoft, I no longer had those wise and kindly nuns and teachers around to set aside dedicated time for me to exist in stillness. During those years, I found the same communion with myself elsewhere— usually during the second half of a long, sweaty jog. Jogging, in those years, was my solace. At Microsoft, which was a real pressure cooker back then, my boss used to hate that my colleague Charlotte and I insisted on going out for a late-afternoon run every day. Too bad, I told her, because without these runs, I'd never last here. (She eventually came around.)

The first part of each run was about pushing ourselves hard and fast, attaining a speed I could never have maintained. That sprint cleared my mind for what came next. As the frantic energy of the day began to burn off and my pace began to slow, I would feel myself entering a more openhearted space. Eventually, I would begin to hear my inner voice breaking through, offering me guidance, encouragement, and often even useful ideas that I could bring back to the office.

Then, when I was in my forties, I found a new way to cultivate stillness. While watching Jon Kabat-Zinn videos on YouTube—and working with the spiritual group some friends and I had formed—I discovered meditation. Meditation can be an intimidating concept, so I appreciated Kabat-Zinn's extremely accessible definition of it. Meditation, he says, is "simply about being yourself and knowing something about who that is." As I began developing my own meditation practice, I learned that by closing my eyes, straightening my back, and focusing my attention on my breath, I was able to carve out a quiet refuge inside myself—my own private chapel—where I could retreat when I needed to refocus.

I guess I sort of assumed that this supportive, encouraging inner voice would stay with me forever, continuing to mature and accrue wisdom and confidence as I did. Instead, something closer to the opposite happened. In the decade or so before my marriage fell apart, my inner voice faded. With it, I lost my center, an essential part of myself. Though I didn't realize it quite yet, I was going to need serious help to get back in touch with the person I used to be, the version of myself that felt truest.

My first step toward getting that help had come when

a close friend pulled me aside one day to pose a gentle question. She knew that I was having difficulties in my marriage and that I was feeling stretched thin between my job at the foundation and the needs of my three children. On top of it all, I was in the throes of a major work problem that was creating a lot of disruption in my life. I spent a lot of time in those days feeling, as I often put it, like my hair was on fire.

"You know, I think you'd find some support helpful," my friend told me in a kind voice. "Are you talking to a therapist?"

I wasn't. Frankly, the idea hadn't even occurred to me. In the Catholic community where I grew up, therapy wasn't really a thing. If you had a problem to work through, you talked to a friend—or maybe, if it was something really serious, the parish priest.

Of course, by this point in my life, I'd been away from that world for some thirty years. I knew plenty of people who'd gone to therapy—people who swore by it, even. When my own loved ones were struggling with something, I had no hesitation whatsoever about suggesting they try therapy. But when my friend brought it up that day, I realized that, at some level, I still thought of therapy as something for *other people*. Thankfully, she helped me see it differently. When she asked me to consider it, I said I would.

Six sessions, I thought. Maybe eight. A quick fix. A new set of tools to help solve a workplace problem that had overstayed its welcome. Maybe I'd stick it out a year, until the problem at work had been resolved and things were back to normal. Then I'd go on my merry way.

I got a referral, made an appointment, and went in mission-driven, intent on getting this work issue behind me and moving on. But the sessions never really went anywhere, and after a few I started to make excuses to postpone or cancel our meetings. Then, around New Year's Day 2014, I received an unmistakable signal that my half-hearted approach to therapy wasn't working: I had a panic attack.

Up until that winter, panic attacks had fortunately been pretty rare events for me. In fact, I think I'd had only one, on a 2006 family vacation to Kenya, in a hot-air balloon hovering about two thousand feet above the Maasai Mara. I was in one part of the balloon's basket with my daughter Jenn when I noticed my seven-year-old son Rory over on the other side, looking like he was about to tip out over the edge. For a heart-stopping moment, I was positive I was about to watch my son die.

Bill grabbed Rory in time, though, pulling him back by his little blue fleece jacket. And, in fact, not only was

Rory totally fine, I'm not even sure he was ever really in danger. (They wouldn't let kids on those things if it were possible for them to just hop out, right?) But for those few seconds when I saw him nearing the edge, I was so terrified that I was about to watch my sweet, curious little boy plunge out of the balloon that even after the moment passed, I couldn't stop shaking. I held myself together— barely—until the balloon landed and everyone had two feet planted firmly on the surface of the earth. Then I went behind a Jeep, crouched down in the tall yellow grass, and screamed. I screamed until my mouth was dry and my throat was raw.

At least my next panic attack had the decency to strike while I was at sea level. Bill and I were in Mexico, at a restaurant by the water, celebrating our twentieth wedding anniversary over lunch. We were actually having a pretty nice time until work came up—as it so often does when you work with your spouse—and that led to a conversation about the topic that was causing me so much stress.

The issue centered on a person we worked with who was, in a word, toxic. It had gotten so bad that a few valued employees had chosen to quit rather than continue working with him. At long last, we had decided to show this guy the door. But when Bill told me what he wanted to give him as an exit package, my jaw dropped.

Bill knew exactly how I felt about this person. And the

fact that he wanted to reward him so extravagantly made me feel incredibly disrespected and disregarded. I *hated* how that guy was treating his colleagues. So when Bill proposed this lavish exit package, I lost it. I felt like the walls were closing in.

I clumsily stumbled to my feet and lunged for the door, the napkin from my lap floating down to the ground behind me. Gasping for air outside, alone, my shoes filling with sand, I was forced to acknowledge that I needed to try something new.

That's when I called someone I trusted and asked for a referral to a new psychologist.

⁓

In retrospect, it's almost funny how wrong I was about the role therapy would play in my life. Because while the first therapist I saw didn't work out, the second one changed everything. I still see her almost every week—*ten years later.*

Going in, I think I had two important misconceptions about therapy, the first being that it was transactional. I went in looking for a solution to this one specific problem that was causing me so much grief. I thought therapy was a product, not a process.

My second misconception was that a therapist would try to lead me around by the nose, taking charge of my life and telling me what to do. I was definitely not in the market for that. So, during our first appointment, I even went so far as to explicitly tell her, "I don't want to be led around by the nose."

Far from being offended, she was amused. "Well," she said, "I'm glad to hear it. Because that is *definitely* not my job. I am not here to tell you what to do."

"Good," I said. "I also don't want to be judged."

"That's not my job, either."

Reassured, I forged ahead. "I'm here," I told her, "because I'm having a lot of difficulty with a personnel issue at work, and it's spilling over into my life outside of it."

This, of course, was completely wrong. But I was absolutely convinced it was the truth.

My therapist, God bless her, just smiled and nodded. It probably only took about one ounce of her extensive training to see that the problem I was there to talk about wasn't *actually* a work problem that was spilling over into my home life. It was a problem *at home* that was spilling over into work. She didn't lecture me, though. She was patient and kind and understanding. And she let me come to the right conclusion myself. Within a few sessions, we'd shifted almost entirely away from talking about what was going on at the office, as important as that was, and begun exploring what was happening at home instead.

Therapy isn't the same for everyone. Sometimes, a handful of sessions *is* all it takes to help someone develop the problem-solving skills they need to change behavioral patterns that are no longer serving them. And sometimes, success requires delving deep into long-held trauma to dig out repressed memories.

For me, it was somewhere in between. What's indisputable, though, is that I needed more help than I thought. Without years of my wonderful therapist's wisdom and guidance, I would never have found my inner voice again. And I certainly never would have had the courage to trust it that winter day in New Mexico when it told me what I had to do.

Therapy made it possible for me to respond to the betrayals in my marriage without betraying myself in return.

⁓

On the last night of that late February 2020 trip to New Mexico, I sat Bill down on the couch. Tomorrow morning, I told him, we're going to fly home to Seattle. But once we get there, it's time for us to begin living separately. Me in our house with Phoebe, our youngest, who was in her last year of high school. And Bill somewhere else.

It was one of the scariest conversations I'd ever had. As angry as I was, as disappointed as I was, as *exhausted* as I was, I was still worried about what this would do to the man who had been my partner in life and work and parenthood for almost thirty years. And yet, as soon as I said it out loud, I knew it was true: I needed space, and I needed time.

Bill, as I anticipated, was sad and upset. He was also understanding and respectful. Frankly, I sensed he was even a little relieved that I was only talking about a separation, not a divorce. I knew the statistics—most couples who separate go on to divorce—but I just wasn't ready to use that word yet. It was too painful a thought to even sit with for very long.

Immediately after I went back to the bedroom to start packing for the trip home, I realized that I already felt less frightened. I had taken a first tentative step into the unknown, and I was ready to see where the transition would take me.

Oddly enough, the first place it took me was right back to Bill. Starting that Monday morning, we were scheduled to be in the same room together for a week of high-stakes meetings at the foundation. In a way, it was good to be thrust right back into a conference room with him. It kept things normal. We hadn't driven to the foundation together like we normally would have, but we quickly proved we were perfectly capable of sitting next to each other in a meeting, focused on work we both cared about.

Then again, there was nothing normal at all about what was happening outside that room. It was March now—March 2020. Near the end of the week, our chief legal officer came in with the foundation security team and presented us with a recommendation that we begin closing our offices to stop the spread of a recently emerged respiratory virus we'd been closely tracking called COVID-19.

It was the beginning of a transition for all of us. As the coronavirus pandemic changed lives around the world overnight, suddenly *everyone*, everywhere around the world, was thrust into a season of fear and uncertainty. I knew so many people who were contending with all kinds of difficult circumstances. People who were sick. Colleagues at the foundation who were trying to stay on top of important work while also teaching multiple grades of home school or taking care of toddlers. Women I'd met from India to Indonesia who made their livings in the informal economy and were now out of work without the safety net of insurance or a savings account. Just a few weeks into the pandemic, the United Nations started warning about a "shadow pandemic" of domestic violence taking place behind closed doors.

Due to the foundation's years of work on pandemic preparedness and our role in the global effort to develop a vaccine, we were suddenly even busier than normal and frequently in the spotlight. (Eventually, we also became the subject of some pretty disturbing disinformation.) Especially during those early weeks—with the pandemic tearing across the globe—Bill and I were both doing a lot of media appearances, sometimes *joint* media appearances. Very few people, even on our own teams, knew we were living apart.

One of those appearances took place just weeks after our separation had begun. Bill and I met up to dial into a Zoom interview, squeezed together shoulder-to-shoulder in front of the camera lens. We'd seen each other at work since our return from Santa Fe, but crowding into the same tight camera shot was a little different. *Nobody watching this has any idea how awkward this is right now*, I thought.

Mostly, though, our COVID-era separation played out behind closed doors, which gave me a lot of room to reflect on the journey that had brought us here—and many quiet hours to hear the voice in my head continue to gather force and strength. That voice wasn't done speaking yet. The question was what I was going to do about what it was telling me.

⁓

"It starts," Oprah Winfrey told me last year in New York, "with a whisper." But if you ignore that whisper, she cautioned, "it comes thumping you on the head, and that thump turns into a problem." From there, she said, it just escalates: "Problems turn into crises, and crises turn into disasters."

As spring of 2020 turned into midsummer, I was slowly becoming more and more convinced that in order to avoid a disaster of my own, I was going to need to summon the courage to tell Bill that I wanted a divorce.

It was incredibly destabilizing to find myself in that position. I had never, ever imagined that I was someone who would get divorced. My three siblings are all in stable, happy marriages. My parents have been married for sixty-three years! I had spent almost my entire adult life invested in this man and our family. After all of that, to contemplate approaching my sixtieth birthday single, on my own? It seemed unthinkable—until, gradually, it didn't.

At some point, I noticed that, quietly, my default assumption had changed. Once, I had wondered, *How could I possibly leave?* Now, I wondered, *How can I possibly stay?*

I didn't travel a straight line to the answer. There were days when I was certain I knew what I wanted to do, followed by days when I was no longer sure. There were days when I felt confident I'd reached a final decision, and days when I went back on what I'd decided.

With the clarity of hindsight, I think it's fair to say that even through this excruciatingly circular decision-making process, my *inner* voice was clear and unequivocal that I needed to get out of my marriage. It was the *other* voices that made me doubt it—voices around me that asked a lot of questions starting with *But what about?*

But what about the kids, one of whom was still under eighteen? But what about our foundation? What about having to tell my family? I didn't really care what the news coverage would be like or what the headlines would say, but the thought of telling my very Catholic parents was horrible.

And then there was the other complicating factor, maybe the most complicated of them all: I loved Bill. Not only that, but I valued our family life deeply—*and* I felt enormous responsibility to the foundation we'd started together. Was I going to rip all that apart? Was I going to forgo the future we'd imagined for so long?

There's a video of us at our wedding reception, all dressed up, about to do the ceremonial cutting of the cake—a tiered wedding cake with a cardboard center. A few seconds into the video, though, I realize Bill doesn't know what he's supposed to do. Instead of cutting one piece and feeding me a single bite like every other groom in history, he thought he was supposed to cut a piece for *everyone*. You can just see him doing his light-speed mental math to decide how big each slice should be.

When I figured out what he was doing, I burst out laughing so hard I couldn't talk. In the video, I'm laughing so hard I'm doubled over. He's looking at me with this confused little smile because he can tell he's gotten something wrong, but he doesn't understand what, and I'm laughing too hard to tell him. Every time he looks at me, I just laugh more, clinging to him, too racked with giggles to stand up straight. Then he starts laughing because I'm laughing, even though he also looks kind of busy, because he still thinks he's supposed to cut 110 pieces of cake.

I used to watch that video almost every year around our anniversary, because it brought me right back into one of the happiest nights of my life. It captures so many of the things I loved about him. Here's this charming, well-meaning, mind-bogglingly brilliant nerd, all dressed up in his tux, just trying to have a good time at the party, happy because I'm happy even though he doesn't exactly know why.

Watching it now brings me to tears.

There are so many more memories where that came from. Three life-changing moments in delivery rooms. Three sets of first words and first steps. Almost thirty years of vacations and holidays and family traditions that we shared. Birthdays. Graduations. Deaths of people we loved and mourned together.

I once told Bill that marriage is like a beautiful crystal bowl, each person holding up one side. Together, over the course of that marriage, you fill that bowl with all sorts of priceless things—all your memories and experiences. When he let go of his side of our bowl, I told him, I couldn't hold it up alone. The whole thing came crashing down, leaving me crouched on the ground, picking up shards, wondering if any of the things we held between us were ever real.

⁓

At the end of the summer of 2020, I drove out to Hood Canal, where Bill was staying, to tell him I'd made a decision. The visit didn't get off to the best start. I was early, and he had a packed morning of video calls. He was flustered as he tried to move his schedule around so we could talk.

I waited. And when he was finished doing what he needed to do, I did what I needed to do: I told him that I wanted a divorce.

We had a long conversation—respectful, not rancorous, even a little tender in moments—and then I got in the car to drive home. On the way back, I pulled over into a parking lot and put on a Willie Nelson song we used to listen to together, "Always on My Mind." I bawled, sobbing over the steering wheel.

But then, when the song ended, I put the car back in motion and drove home.

⁓

The day that followed was even weirder and more painful. I drove back out to Hood Canal so I could check on

Bill and so we could start talking about how we'd tell our kids. Eventually, we got hungry, so we went to get burgers. That part was totally surreal—an out-of-body experience. How many times in our lives had we gone to get a burger together, him driving, me in the passenger seat? It was a scene that had played out hundreds of times between us. But this time, we were talking about how we were going to separate our lives, to move forward into a world where we didn't do these things together anymore. We were jointly planning out a future that we weren't going to share.

I knew the months ahead were going to be difficult. Bill has a reputation for being one of the toughest negotiators in the world. I'd been in the background for some of his exchanges with the Department of Justice in the early nineties, and I was not looking forward to the part where our respective attorneys were going to start carving up the life we'd made together. Once again, I started having panic attacks.

"Melinda, when this happens, you need to call me," my therapist said. "I have training."

I laughed. "These aren't exactly the kinds of things that limit themselves to business hours," I told her.

"I will sleep with my phone by the bed," she told me. "Really," she added when she saw my face. "I've done this for other clients in moments like this, and I'll do it for you. Not forever, but for right now."

But wouldn't I be waking up her husband, too? "He's in the business, Melinda," she told me. "He understands."

Sure enough, there were nights when I took her up on it. Not every night, but some nights. Other times, when I felt the first waves of panic starting to set in, I'd go outside for a sweaty jog, just enough activity to shift my energy and give my anxiety a place to go. When I could, I meditated. And when my mind was too frenzied to focus on the sound of my breath, I listened to audiobooks, letting them relax me to sleep.

Pretty soon, I realized I didn't need to have my therapist sleeping by her phone, available at all hours of the night. With her typical wisdom and gentle touch, she helped me see and believe that I could get myself through this on my own. She helped me create the conditions for my own inner voice, the one that knew me and knew how to comfort and motivate me, to emerge again. I was more in touch with the deepest version of myself than I'd been in years.

⁓

Despite all my inner work, the process of finalizing our divorce was grueling. The negotiations over our agreement took much longer than I'd expected or hoped for. My brother Steven described me as a speedboat tied to the dock, engines revving, pulling and straining against the rope holding it back. "Yeah, but I'm sawing at that big thick rope with a frickin' penknife," I told him one frustrated day.

"Well, keep at it," he told me. "And just remember, eventually you're going to break away. It might not be smooth at first—you might teeter—but then you'll be off and flying."

As for my parents, well, I put off telling them as long as I could. Then came the holidays, and I couldn't keep the secret any longer. I went into the conversation with notes to help guide me, because I knew it would be so difficult. I made the call from a house where I was staying with some friends. Knowing how nervous I was, one of them prayed for me in the garden while another made me a smoothie to drink as soon as the call was over.

My apprehension was misplaced, though. My parents responded with empathy and total support. Although they never thought it was their place to get involved in my marriage, they had noticed things over the years that made them quite understanding of why I needed to get out. Now, I had one less thing to be afraid of.

Once we'd finalized the agreement, Bill and I used the weekend to tell our friend Warren Buffett, a close partner of our foundation, and the foundation's CEO, Mark Suzman. Then, at 1:30 p.m. Pacific time, on Monday, May 3, 2021, Bill and I released a joint statement. "After a great deal of thought and work on our relationship, we have made the decision to end our marriage," we wrote, asking for space and privacy for our family.

As the news started hitting the headlines, I was at home with my younger daughter, Phoebe, who was lying in bed with her phone. At one point, I climbed under the covers to curl around her, cuddling her. She showed me a few of the funny memes the internet created about the divorce announcement, and we laughed a little, but I wasn't really in a celebratory mood. It had been an unbelievably hard stretch, and I was tired and very sad.

I was lucky that year that I had my older daughter Jenn's wedding to look forward to in October. Later that fall, I also managed to rally for a vacation with some close girlfriends that they jokingly dubbed my "freedom tour." But I made a point of not doing any interviews for the rest of the year. I wasn't ready to speak publicly about the divorce yet, so I avoided any situation where it might come up.

It took until the next March for me to find the courage to reclaim my public voice. After a lot of careful consideration, I agreed to do an interview with Gayle King, a journalist I trust and respect. In the weeks leading up to the interview, I prepped—and I prayed. I prayed for grace. I prayed that I would find the words to speak the truth of my experience. I prayed that I would do right by my children in the way I talked about their father. I prayed that I would do right by myself.

Gayle flew out to Seattle for the interview. At the last minute, I had to change clothes when we realized we were wearing the exact same shade of pink. She apologized and explained she'd flown out with only one outfit. I didn't mind. That day, my clothes were the least of my worries. I was channeling every ounce of my energy into what I was going to say.

The obvious question on everyone's mind was *What happened?* There was a lot of speculation about what, exactly, Bill had done to make me leave him. I didn't want to engage with any of it. So I simply said that questions about Bill's role in the events that led up to our divorce were questions for him to answer. I still feel that way.

But it was important to me to speak what was true for me: That I had been absolutely committed to this marriage. That I was proud of the family we'd started and the foundation we'd built. That I was heartbroken. At one point, I told Gayle, "I had a lot of tears for many days, days where I'm literally lying on the floor, the carpet this close to me, thinking, 'How can this be? How can I get up? How am I going to move forward?'" That was definitely not a line I'd practiced—not something I'd ever planned to share so publicly—but it was true. And it made me feel powerful to hear words that even my inner voice could only whisper come out of my mouth for everyone to hear.

After Gayle was done with her questions and the cameras had stopped rolling, I said goodbye and went up to

my office alone. It was gloomy outside—a dark and rainy
Seattle day. But as I sat down at my desk, in my second-
choice outfit and heavy TV makeup, I noticed something
shift inside me. Finally, after all these months, that little
speedboat I'd imagined straining so hard against the dock
was free.

~⌒~

Leaving my marriage was one of the hardest and most important things I've ever done. And there is, I am sure, a
parallel universe where none of this ever happened. Where
I never learned to listen to the voice that whispered inside me. Where I didn't have the people around me who
gave me the courage to do what I needed to do to regain
control over my life and make myself whole again. I am
lucky—so lucky—to have had the teachers I did, the
friends I do, and the therapist who agreed to take me on.

Now, whether I'm talking to young people or other
women my age, I often find myself sharing what I've
learned about how important it is to distill the sound of
your own inner voice—to develop the skills to distinguish
between the scripts you have been handed by others and
the story you are writing for yourself. Often, I tell them,
the first step to turning up the volume of your inner voice
is to put what it's saying to you out into the world. Write it
in your journal. Tell it to your spouse or a friend you trust.

Tell it to someone in your family. Tell it to a therapist. Therapy made all the difference for me, and I hope my experience might encourage some other skeptics out there to consider that it could make a difference for you, too.

These big moments in our lives, these big decision points that become inflection points, start, as Oprah phrased it, with a whisper. And to manage these moments with intention and purpose, we should aim to meet them there, too. "Catch it in the whisper," Oprah says. Ask yourself, she says, "What is whispering to you now?"

What is whispering to you now?

Chapter Five

Pause in the Clearing

The summer after I finished seventh grade, my dad's work sent him away to attend something called the Successful Life Course. The course was taught by a man named Ed Foreman, who, the brochure explained, "rose from the back-breaking toil of a meager farm existence to a financially successful business career in construction, transportation, and petroleum development."

I'll never forget going with my mom and siblings to pick up my dad at the Dallas airport when he returned. The plane arrived at the gate, and this whole cadre of people who had been at the training together practically burst into the terminal, brimming with positive energy. When my dad emerged from the jetway, he stood there, holding his briefcase, and, with the others, proclaimed to everyone within earshot: "I'm happy! I'm healthy! I'm *terrific*!"

Oh my God, I remember thinking. *What did they* do *to my father?*

My family didn't go out to dinner very often (money was tight back then), but that night, Dad took us all to the Old Spaghetti Factory, where he spent the evening raving about the newfound confidence and perspective on life he'd gained from the course. "And, of course," he added, gesturing exuberantly at my sister and me with a piece of bread, "Susan and Melinda are going to go next!"

The nearest course was being taught in a town in East Texas called Kilgore. I'd never been there before, but a few weeks later, my sister and I piled into a van with another family (my father had met their mother at the course), and we all drove down together to get a big dose of motivation.

At the outset of the course, we each got a navy blue binder containing all the materials. "If you will practice the principles of this program," one page promised, "you will INCREASE your PERSONAL EFFECTIVENESS, DRIVE & SUCCESS AT LEAST 30% . . . in many cases 50% to 100%." That sounded pretty good to me, so I paid careful attention and resolved to do whatever Ed Foreman and his team of instructors advised.

They made us read Dale Carnegie. They taught us how to engage in what they called "mind-controlled relaxation" (essentially, power naps). And, most of all, they emphasized the importance of goal setting. In the back of that navy blue binder was a sheaf of blank loose-leaf paper on which we were told to write down our life goals. And we had to promise that, each night before bed, we would review the list and then copy it over onto a fresh sheet of paper, just to make sure we were truly committed.

As a rule follower, I dutifully sat down to make my list in neat blue cursive handwriting.

I started with a few things I wanted to achieve by the time I turned thirteen. Long fingernails. A spot on student council. And I wanted to be asked to the graduation dance, preferably by one of two specific boys I'd set my sights on.

I then turned to some longer-term goals:

- By age fourteen, I wanted to have made the intramural cheerleading squad.
- By twenty, I wanted to have taken a trip to Europe.
- And by twenty-one, I wanted to own my own car. ("A Cadillac with velvet seats," I specified, dreamily.)

Can you believe I'm telling you about these? Me neither. Reading them over definitely makes me cringe. And while I don't know if these particular goals were exactly what Ed Foreman had in mind, the practice of goal setting stuck with me long after the course ended. Late at night, I would pull out that navy blue binder, sit down at the little desk in my bedroom, and carefully add to the list. Over time, the goals I wrote down started to become more and more serious.

For example, in my freshman year of high school, I decided that I wanted to be accepted to Notre Dame, the Catholic university I'd long dreamed of attending, but also to Duke and maybe one day to Stanford for graduate school like my dad. I already knew that getting into one of those schools would require more than straight A's: I'd have to be at the very top of Ursuline Academy's class of 1982. So, in between "I want to be able to talk to guys easier" and "Make the drill team the best it has ever been," I wrote, "Make Valedictorian!"

Part of the Successful Life Course was about going back to these goals and reflecting on the ones we'd achieved. I wasn't so dutiful about that part. I would occasionally review old lists and cross out items I had accomplished— scratching out "be on student council" when I managed to get myself elected and jubilantly scrawling "I did it!!!" next to "dance with John W. at a party." But for the most part, as soon as I was done with one goal, my entire focus would shift to the next one. Even when I did eventually make valedictorian, I spent approximately five seconds feeling good about it. Then I got so worried about the next task—figuring out what I would say in my graduation speech—that I started to cry.

What's more, I never really took the time to think about whether the next goal on my list was still the *right* goal—or to evaluate whether it was something I even wanted anymore. Once I decided that I needed to learn to speed-read or exactly how much I should weigh by a given date, that was the plan, and I was sticking to it! I just kept pressing forward.

Looking back all these decades later, I can't help but wince a little at what I missed out on during all those years. The girl I see when I page through that binder was driven by a mix of ambition and anxiety. Yes, I got a lot done. But I also missed opportunities to embrace spontaneity, lean into the unexpected, and learn something new about myself and the world.

I think about it this way: Most of the time, we walk through life in the thicket of our everyday routine. We're in familiar surroundings, but we're so boxed in that it can be hard to see the full landscape. In moments of transition, though, we step into a clearing in our lives. The familiar surroundings disappear. In these big wide-open spaces, there's a lot of uncertainty—but also a lot of possibility.

I've learned that there are two ways to encounter these spaces. You can keep your head down and focus on finding the shortest possible distance to the next familiar thing, racing past the unknown without a second glance. Or you can find the courage to pause in that in-between space and see what it has to tell you—and then let what you learn there help you decide where to go next.

For the first part of my life, I was the person with her head down, darting between familiar things, rushing toward something I'd already decided I wanted even before I fully understood the whole spectrum of options before me. It's taken me most of my life to find the courage to keep my heart open to what exists in these in-between spaces, to treat the unfamiliar as a teacher instead of an enemy.

I remained an obsessive goal setter well into adulthood. In college, I'd come home during breaks, pull that old blue binder down off my bookshelf, and add new goals to the list: get an MBA, intern at IBM, work at a tech company, eventually start a business of my own. As it turned out, my maniacal focus on plowing forward to the next thing actually made me a great fit when I started working at Microsoft, because that's how everyone else there operated, too.

But maybe being surrounded by people who took my own goal-oriented tendencies to such an extreme was the wake-up call I needed. Because during my time at Microsoft, something inside me began to change. I occasionally found myself sneaking out of the office after major product launches for long contemplative drives along Lake Sammamish, or even taking entire days off (verboten at Microsoft back then) to rest and regroup after a big project got done. Even if just for a short period of time, I was stopping to savor the accomplishment and be present with the transition into the next thing.

Make no mistake: I was still a young woman in an enormous hurry. And it's not like I was being intentional about using that time to truly reflect on where I was in life and where I wanted to go from there. Still, I was beginning to feel just a tiny bit less beholden to the inexorable pull of whatever item came next on the list.

Another turning point came when, for the first time, I made a conscious decision to abandon one of the big goals on my list: moving home. After getting my dream job at an exciting tech company (check!), I had always planned to go back to Dallas to be near my family. When I moved out to Seattle after graduation for my job, I had no intention of staying there. Seattle was never part of my long-term plan.

In fact, it's hard to think of two cities more different than Dallas and Seattle. In Dallas, it felt as if everyone was always dressed to the nines and no one left the house without their hair curled. ("The higher the hair, the closer to God," as they say.) In Seattle, most people dress like they're on their way to go hiking—and given all the mountains and lakes and stunning natural beauty, you hope they are. In Dallas, the weather is warm and the people are warmer. (Texans are extremely friendly.) In Seattle, it's dark all winter, and it can take a while to get to know people. (There's something called "the Seattle freeze.") If you're out running errands in Dallas, someone you meet is probably going to call you "sweetheart." In Seattle, no way.

To my total surprise, though, I found myself beginning to take root in my new surroundings. I started hiking, learned how to ski, and got addicted to kayaking—things that were never on my radar before I moved to Seattle and certainly didn't appear on any list of goals I'd ever made. What's more, when I was twenty-seven, the stock I'd lucked into as an early Microsoft employee made it possible for me to do something else—something big— that *definitely* wasn't on the list: I bought a house, a small bungalow in a Seattle neighborhood called Leschi, on the western shore of Lake Washington. I still remember how much fun I had going to the garden store on the weekends, selecting items to make it feel like home.

I think a younger me would have been shocked at the thought of settling into a home somewhere that wasn't Dallas. And yet, there I was, finally putting the list aside so I could make room for something new, something that I hadn't known to plan for. It turned out to be one of the happiest times of my life—not *despite* the fact that I had abandoned my carefully laid plans to move home to Dallas but precisely *because* I had allowed the unexpected to seize control of my path. After all that careful goal setting, one of the most important milestones in my twenties—buying that home—was one I'd never anticipated.

A few years ago, Woo-kyoung Ahn, a psychology professor at Yale, wrote a book called *Thinking 101*. In the book, she introduces readers to Max Hawkins, a former Google employee who, one day, decided to hand control of his life over to an algorithm. More specifically, Max built an app that would automatically call an Uber to take him to a location randomly picked from a Google listing without him knowing where he was going. He would just get in the car when it arrived at his house and see where he wound up.

For many people, this probably sounds like a nightmare. But for Max, committing to serendipity was addictive. "He started discovering random florists, grocery stores, and bars he never knew existed," writes Dr. Ahn, "because, thinking that his life was pretty well set, he'd never explored his options." Eventually, Max expanded his app to include public events announced on Facebook, and he would show up at whatever random event the app spat out, which led him to a diverse set of activities including "drinking White Russians with Russian people, attending an AcroYoga class, and staying for five hours at a party thrown by a retired psychologist he had never met." And he had a great time!

"Life is indeed full of possibilities," Dr. Ahn concludes, "and it's up to you to discover them." You can't do that if you're blinded by your focus on getting to the next item on your list. The more certain we are of what our life should be like, the more limited we are by our imagination.

∽

During the week of Valentine's Day 2022—my first Valentine's Day since finalizing my divorce—I was scanning *New York Times* headlines on my phone when I came across a contributed essay entitled "Marriage Made Me Let Go of My Dreams. Good." With that headline, you bet I clicked. And I was glad I did.

The essay was by the frequent *New York Times* contributor Reverend Esau McCaulley, a writer and theologian. Behind the clickbaity title, I discovered a beautiful meditation on opening your heart, letting go of your plans, and reconceptualizing your dreams.

Reverend McCaulley writes that he knew from the age of six that he wanted to be a pastor when he grew up. He opens the piece by explaining that becoming a pastor was not only his dream, but his inheritance:

If you visit the cemetery on the plantation that hosts the graves of my mother's side of the family, you will see names with "Reverend" etched into the tombstones going all the way back to the 1800s. My ancestors, slaves and later tenant farmers, would leave the cotton fields after a long day of work, put on their best pair of overalls and preach the good news to other weary Black folks looking for a modicum of hope.

But then, as a young seminarian, he fell in love with a woman. Not just any woman, but an aspiring pediatrician who had been dreaming of joining the Navy for as long as he had wanted to be a pastor. And as they contemplated their lives together, they realized those two dreams were fundamentally in conflict. A pastor must have deep roots in a congregation and community. A Navy doctor signs up for a life of moving their family from base to base.

That meant that to marry the woman he loved, Reverend McCaulley had to agree to let the life he'd imagined for himself as a child fall away. But he doesn't spend the essay mourning the loss of that life. Indeed, he argues that letting it go was a good thing. "Few of us become everything that we dreamed," he writes. "One reason is that our dreams often can be shockingly selfish."

This, I thought, was an insightful perspective. As a society, we often ascribe a certain virtue to people's lifelong dreams, as if those are, for some reason, more authentic or worthwhile than the dreams and aspirations we develop later in life. The truth, though, as Reverend McCaulley explains, is that there's important value in being willing to change your plans as your understanding of the world expands and grows more complex. Sometimes, the best thing you can do for yourself and the people around you is to have the wisdom to know which dreams to let go of in order to make room for something new. Some dreams undoubtedly propel us forward, but others hold us back. The trick is learning to distinguish between the two— and, when you decide an old dream no longer serves you, finding the courage to slip its bonds.

⁓

It was my good friend Charlotte whose wise counsel helped me put away the navy blue binder once and for all.

Several years ago, on one of our regular walks, I was going on about my latest self-improvement goal, and I noticed she was being very quiet. Charlotte had heard a lot of this from me over the years, but this time she wasn't giving me the usual encouragement. Instead, she paused on the walking path we were on and said, gently, "Melinda, you've squeezed every bit of juice out of the turnip." It was time, she told me, to stop cramming so much onto my plate—so many goals, so many tasks, so much anxiety.

Instead of darting across the clearing to the next thing, I needed to pause and just be.

My younger self likely would have dismissed her advice. But maybe because I'd known her for so long (we met at work eight weeks after I started at Microsoft in 1987), and maybe because she's such a type A goal setter herself, I let her point sink in. It probably also helped that we'd recently been talking a lot about the concept of liminal space—the intermediate zone between where we've been and where we're going—a topic that came up again and again in the work of the meditation teachers we were studying, including the beloved psychologist Dr. Tara Brach.

In her book *Radical Acceptance*, Brach describes the Buddhist concept of the sacred pause, writing, "A pause is a suspension of activity, a time of temporary disengagement when we are no longer moving toward any goal." These pauses, she says, "can last for an instant, for hours, or for seasons of our life." What makes them so important, she explains, is that pausing helps us become "absolutely available to the changing stream of life" instead of closing ourselves off to possibility.

All of this proved to be invaluable advice and impeccably timed. Not long afterward, I found myself facing an extremely unexpected series of transitions that I couldn't have planned for if I'd tried: In 2020, I made the decision to end my marriage. In 2021, I finalized my divorce. And in 2024, I left the foundation I'd helped build, the center of my life's work.

Even just a year before this all began, I don't think I would have predicted that a single one of those changes was on the horizon. In fact, in April of 2019, I was asked in an interview, "Who or what is the greatest love of your life?" and the answer came to me in a heartbeat. "It's an unbreakable tie," I said, "between the foundation we started, the man I started it with, and the three children we have together." The answer felt so obvious and fundamental that it required no thought at all. And yet, just five years later, I found myself preparing to enter a world where I had severed ties with both Bill *and* our foundation.

I've already described the long road to my decision to end my marriage. But even after Bill and I were no longer married, my plan was to continue on together as cochairs of the Gates Foundation. I care very deeply about the work the foundation is doing in the United States and around the world. I never, ever imagined that I would step away from that.

But in the end, I did. That's because it wasn't just my relationship to Bill that had changed. The world around me was changing, too. After a difficult few years of watching women's rights rolled back (the Supreme Court's decision to overturn *Roe v. Wade*, to name just one deeply troubling example), I realized it was time to move forward into the next chapter of my philanthropy—and to focus that chapter on helping to alter the trajectory for women and girls in the United States and around the world. I am simply not willing to accept the idea that my granddaughters could grow up with less freedom than I had. And I knew that by leaving the foundation, I would have more time and resources to devote to this fight—as well as, for the first time in my philanthropic career, full control over how those resources were used.

Even so, leaving wasn't easy. In the weeks leading up to the announcement, I thought a lot about all the people whose work might be disrupted by my departure. That was my biggest hesitation—that I would let down people who were depending on me. My colleagues. The foundation's grantees. And most important, the people whose lives are touched by our work. In the end, though, I realized that what the foundation does is much bigger than any one person, and between our board and our CEO, I would be leaving it in extremely capable hands.

I'll never forget the moment before I sent Bill the email about my decision. I had told very few people what I was about to do, and as I prepared to press Send, one of them, a close adviser, asked me a final time if I was sure. We both knew that as soon as the email was sent, one very important chapter of my life would be over forever. "Yes, I am," I said to her. "I'm ready." A fraction of a second later, my note was in Bill's inbox.

Bill wrote back quickly to say he was sad to hear this and asked if there was anything he could do to convince me to stay. I said no, that my mind was made up. My last day of work at the foundation, I told him, would be June 7, 2024.

Back in 2015, I had started another organization, Pivotal, which focuses on dismantling barriers that hold people back, with a particular focus on women, especially women of color. For almost a decade, I'd split my time between Pivotal and the Gates Foundation. Now, Pivotal would become my new home base and the center of all my work.

Even before I announced that I was leaving the foundation, I had some ideas of what my next chapter could look like, but I also wanted to take things slowly and wait to commit the majority of my resources until I'd had a lot of time to consider options. Because if there's one thing I've learned during my career in philanthropy, it's that I don't have all the answers—not even close. I feel more and more humble about my role all the time and more convinced than ever that I make myself most useful to the world by standing behind movements led by others rather than trying to start movements myself.

Some of that was a bit of a shift for me. When Bill and

I first decided to give away the majority of our wealth, we wrote a public letter in which we laid out our priorities. "We want to make sure lifesaving vaccines reach everyone who needs them," we wrote, "and that the world develops new vaccines." We added that we wanted to work on expanding access to education and health care because "we believe that every child deserves the chance to grow up, to dream and do big things."

After we divorced, I wrote another public letter recommitting to giving away the majority of my wealth, and, again, I laid out my clear intention to "commit my time, energy, and efforts to the work of fighting poverty and advancing equality—for women and girls and other marginalized groups—in the United States and around the world."

But then I added something that was important to me:

It's much easier to imagine that you have all the answers when you're sitting in a conference room in Seattle than when you're face-to-face with a business owner in Nairobi or an indigenous activist in New Mexico who is telling you in her own words about her hopes for the future and the challenges she sees to realizing them. That's why I think philanthropy is most effective when it prioritizes flexibility over ideology—and why I'll continue to seek out new partners, ideas, and perspectives.

When I left the foundation, I decided to be even more intentional about putting those values into action. It would have felt like such a waste to enter that wide-open space in front of me with my path already mapped out. Why not, instead, keep myself open to the new people and ideas that will be crossing through and to all that I can learn from them? I have no doubt that people I haven't yet met and things I haven't yet learned will turn out to play critical roles in the next phase of Pivotal's work. The most important part of my job right now is seeking out people with lived experience of the issues I care about and being open to following them where they lead me.

Not long ago, my son, Rory, told me that every time he meets someone new, he tries to listen for two things they say that could make him change his mind about something. I so deeply admire his commitment to challenging his assumptions and looking to each and every person he meets as someone with something to teach him. One thing I want to do in my next chapter is be more like Rory.

I was a few months away from announcing my plans to leave the foundation when, in January 2024, a surprising email popped up in my inbox. It was from Stanford University—an invitation to speak at the commencement ceremony that June.

In recent years, I'd received a lot of communications from Stanford's campus. Most of them, though, were from my daughter Phoebe, then a Stanford junior studying human biology, calling to say her bike had been stolen again. (Phoebe went through a lot of bikes.)

Stanford has long held a special place in my family's heart because of that scholarship my father received to study there. The school became even dearer to us when my daughters, Jenn and Phoebe, chose Stanford for their own undergraduate educations. Jenn's husband, Nayel, is a Stanford graduate as well. The invitation intrigued me even before I noticed that commencement that year was scheduled for Father's Day, which felt especially fitting given my dad's history with the school.

Before I considered accepting, though, I called Phoebe to ask what she thought. No way was I showing up on her campus in a role like that without talking it through with her first. Phoebe was thrilled for me and insisted I say yes. A few days later, she called back to share some exciting news of her own: She'd arranged to graduate early and would receive her diploma the same day as my speech. Somehow, she'd squeezed in extra coursework while at the same time preparing to launch a business and emerging as a forceful advocate for women's reproductive rights. (She also, I have no doubt, managed to pack a full four years of parties into her abbreviated time on campus. From the days when she was a toddler in her car seat, she used to tell us, "Good thing I'm here, because without me, this family would be *so boring*.")

Once I told Stanford how honored I would be to be its commencement speaker, it was time to write a speech—and just like in the moments after I found out I was high school valedictorian, I felt a bit daunted by the assignment. Commencement speeches are always hard. Here's an audience of incredibly brilliant and accomplished people, and they're looking to you to convey some sort of advice they haven't heard before. And, of course, this invitation came at a particularly strange time in my own life.

I decided to treat it as an opportunity to learn. I emailed Stanford back to ask if I could speak with the class presidents to find out what was on their minds as they prepared for this massive transition of their own. The university set up a Zoom call, and it proved to be even more valuable than I could have imagined.

One of the class presidents told me that he'd noticed that many of his classmates felt that because they were Stanford students, they had to conform to a certain mold and to meet a certain set of expectations about the kind of job or career they were "supposed" to pursue, the kind of lives they were "supposed" to lead, the kind of people they were "supposed" to become. When I asked him what he thought they needed to hear, he urged me to encourage them to set themselves free from such a narrow set of expectations.

That sounded right—and, what's more, it sounded like a powerful message for new graduates and, for that matter, just about anyone.

Nine days after my last day of work at the foundation, I woke up near Palo Alto, got dressed and ready with Phoebe, and drove over to Stanford's campus, where I donned my regalia and took my seat onstage. When it was my turn to speak, I asked the students to let their degree be the beginning, not the end, of their process of self-discovery.

"You are Stanford students," I told them, "so I imagine most of you are graduating today with big plans for yourselves. Higher degrees to earn, causes to advance, companies to start, industries to disrupt. These big, bold plans are wonderful. The world needs you."

And then I gave them the very advice—the very pep talk—I had needed so often throughout that season myself:

But my advice is to leave some room for those plans to change. Resist the idea that anything you've done here at Stanford has already locked you into any one path—or any one kind of life or career. Be excited about the fact that you will encounter possibilities you haven't imagined yet. And be willing to let what you learn shift your thinking about what you're on this earth to do.

I have no doubt that many of those young people were like I was at their age—driven, ambitious, and motivated to achieve as much as possible in life. I would even bet that more than a few of them had lists of goals of their own, tucked away in notebooks or glued to a vision board. And there's nothing wrong with that, nothing wrong with being ambitious or even capturing those ambitions on a list like the one Ed Foreman taught us to make all those years ago.

I've learned, however—even if it took me decades to learn it—that it's worth leaving some space between the lines of those lists. Space for spontaneity and fun and joy. Space for new ideas and new people. And, most of all, space for its own sake, because when transitions come—and they will come—we need to be ready to spend a bit of time in the clearings in our lives they create.

After all, transitions are disruptive and disorienting. They lay waste to all our careful planning and force us to question our assumptions, our ambitions, even our very identities. But that, I've come to understand, is part of their magic.

Chapter Six

Plant Roots

Even though it's been nearly fifty years since I last set foot inside the greeting-card store near my childhood home in Dallas, I can still close my eyes and conjure the whole sensory experience of the place. The bell that jingled when you opened the door. The cozy fall-candle smell in the air—florals and cinnamon. The warm greetings from the two elderly ladies who worked there.

When I was growing up, my mother, Elaine, was always dipping in and out of that store, Happy Happy Hallmark, my siblings and me in tow. The fact that I remember it so vividly is a testament to Mom and the thoughtfulness that kept her returning there again and again, leaving each time with cards to mark every possible occasion in the lives of the people she cared about. Birthdays. First Communions. Graduations. Weddings. Deaths.

If something important was happening to you, you could count on my mother to be there with a card. My siblings and I spent hours of our lives looking at toys and stickers while my mother patiently searched for exactly the right expression of comfort, congratulations, or condolence. To this day, Mom still sends cards to mark special occasions and joyfully receives many cards from our family and her friends in return.

All those cards my mom has sent over her lifetime say a lot about the kind of woman she is. But it occurs to me that they also reveal something about their recipients. If you were to stack up all the cards you've ever received from my mother, they would tell the story of your life, plotting out a rough map of the transitions that have defined you. Milestones at school and work. Weddings and new babies. Illnesses and heartbreaks. Through it all, my mother's cards were her way of letting you know that she was thinking of you and that she believed these moments in your life deserved to be acknowledged.

Her sense of occasion translated into other parts of our family life, too. Our birthdays were one example. We didn't do big presents or anything like that. (In fact, on more than one occasion, I ripped open the wrapping paper on my birthday gift only to find school supplies, the downside of being born in August.) Still, there would always be a party, with streamers and balloons and a cake—and, of course, a card.

My mother also made a huge deal out of the winter holidays. Every year, my parents assembled their artificial Christmas tree from Sears, Roebuck, and Company in our living room, the "fanciest" room in our house. Most of the time, that room was strictly off-limits to my siblings and me, but as long as the Christmas tree was up, we were allowed to come and go as we pleased. My sister, Susan, and I spent many pleasant December hours lying on the floor in the glow of the lights, soaking up the magic of it all.

The holiday spirit was allowed into every room of my maternal grandparents' house in New Orleans, too. During the rest of the year, my grandmother was somewhat particular about who could be where. But one Christmas, she even let us test out our new roller skates in her hallway, right on her shiny terrazzo floors. I couldn't tell you the last time I strapped on a roller skate, but I remember exactly how wickedly delighted we all were to be roller-skating *inside* at *Grandma's*.

Now that I have three children of my own, it's clear to me that my mom and her mom knew exactly what they were doing. By allowing us to break a few rules during Christmas, they not only ensured we had fun as a family, they also communicated in an age-appropriate way that some occasions are so special that they deserve to transcend the ordinary business of everyday life. Just like her loving efforts on our birthdays—and her insistence that the entire family sign every card she sent—my mother's approach to the holidays was one more way she taught me not to lose sight of what truly matters.

~⌒∘

Imagine, then, how disappointed my mother must have been in me on Jenn's very first Christmas. Even twenty-eight years and many happy holidays together later, the memory of that Christmas Eve still fills me with regret.

Jenn was eight months old at the time, and my parents had flown out to spend the holiday in Southern California with Bill, Jenn, and me. When the morning of Christmas Eve rolled around, Bill wanted to play golf, and he wanted me to go with him. Those of us who live in Seattle don't take winter sunshine for granted, so maybe that's why I didn't put up much resistance. Plus, we would be back in plenty of time for dinner. I grabbed my clubs and jumped in the car with him, leaving Jenn with my parents.

When I got home later that afternoon, I realized the mistake I'd made right away. My mom was in the kitchen, holding my baby daughter, making a special Christmas meal for my family. She was giving Jenn the same beautiful holiday she'd always given my siblings and me. But my daughter's *own* mother had spent the day somewhere else.

My mom didn't say anything about it to me. Neither did my father. They didn't have to. I could see it in their eyes. For my whole life, they had modeled for me that the holidays are a time to be together as a family, an occasion that asks us to step away from the pulls of everyday life to be present for each other instead. And on my very first chance to do for my daughter what they'd always done for me, I left her behind for hours and hours. I missed so much of her first Christmas Eve. To play *golf.*

Even as mad at myself as I was, though, I was grateful that my parents, and my mother in particular, had established such a strong sense of tradition around the holidays that it had forced a reset for me. At their best, rituals and traditions keep us anchored in our values and firmly rooted—in ourselves, in each other, in what's important. By the next day, Christmas Day, I was already back on track.

My education on this topic continued a few months later when, at the recommendation of another young mother I knew, I signed Jenn and me up for a "pretoddler" class at a nearby community college taught by a parent educator named Dee Ann Perea. Jenn is now grown with two children of her own, but I still have a handout from that class entitled "Sharing Rituals and Traditions." At the top, Dee Ann wrote, "Rituals and traditions are heart tending!" and went on to explain, "Experts tell us that these kinds of shared experiences have a profound effect on family life. Rituals help bind us together, give everyone a sense of belonging and create memories."

Underneath the preamble, she wrote out a long list of enthusiastically punctuated ideas for family rituals and traditions to adopt, from "Power out night, picnic in the house with flashlights!" to "Pajama Day! Stay home all day!" to "Eat Breakfast for lunch and lunch for Breakfast!" "Keep in mind," she added, that these family rituals "don't have to be expensive or elaborate. And don't have to always be about happy times."

I absolutely loved that parenting class. And I loved that worksheet because it offered a framework to help me recreate for my own family some of what I'd loved about my childhood. Inspired by my mother and full of new ideas from Dee Ann Perea, I made a point of developing a new set of family traditions for my three kids.

For example, until Phoebe, the youngest of the three, went off to college, we'd observe something I called "closing the doors for Christmas." As soon as the kids were out of school for the holidays, we'd pull back from our usual routines and spend that time on family instead. I found that opting out of the usual distractions made it easier for us to give this special occasion the space in our hearts it deserved.

Once we'd closed the doors for Christmas, we had some days that were full of family activities and others that had no agenda at all. The important thing was that we were together—and that, just like at my parents' and my grandma's, the usual rules didn't apply. When the kids were little and wanted to fill a hall closet with packing peanuts to dive into, I channeled their grandmother and cheered them on. (I just DustBusted them off on their way out so they couldn't track little bits of Styrofoam around the house.) The fact that they still talk about that day is how I know we succeeded in making Christmas a source of treasured memories for them, too.

Like my mom, I also tried to make each birthday in our household a special occasion. The night before, after the birthday boy or girl had gone to sleep, Bill and I would sneak into their room with balloons so they'd wake up to something special. By the time they got home from school, the family room would be decorated, too. We would always have dinner together as a family—per Bill's family tradition, the lucky kid whose birthday we were celebrating would get to pick the menu—followed by cake and presents.

Separately, we'd have the kids' friends over to the house for a big birthday party, always organized around a theme—whether it was "unicorn princess fairies" for a three-year-old Jenn, "Dora the Explorer" for a four-year-old Phoebe, or "mad scientist" for a five-year-old Rory. (A side note: If your kid ever asks for a reptile-themed birthday party—looking at you again, Rory—don't hire the guy who brings over real, live reptiles. The kids will be freaked out, and now a guy who travels around with real, live reptiles knows where you live.)

We developed another birthday tradition that revolves around a special hat. After so many years of following my mom around Happy Happy Hallmark, I have a soft spot for little gift shops. One day when Jenn was little, I was poking around one of those shops when I came across an oversized hat with fabric birthday candles sticking out of the top. *Well*, I thought, *that's definitely coming home with me.* Since then, if you live in my house and it is your birthday, you *will* wear that hat—and as far as I'm concerned, you will wear it all day long. (Although once, on Jenn's birthday, an enthusiastic but slightly confused Bill thought *he* was the one who was supposed to wear the hat, which raised some eyebrows at school drop-off that morning.) Over the years, that goofy hat has traveled all over the world with us.

I also tried to incorporate a sense of ritual into the 360 days a year that *weren't* the birthday of anyone in our immediate family. Starting when Jenn was quite little, we'd all go around the dinner table and name something we were grateful for. When I first proposed the idea to Bill, he wasn't totally sold. While I'd grown up saying grace before dinner, his family got straight to the food, so he worried it would feel stiff and forced. Plus, he thought that at three years old, Jenn might be too young to get it. But the first night we tried it, she ended up being the one to convince him herself, and all it took was four words: "I'm thankful for *Daddy*." With that, another tradition became firmly established.

Some nights, the kids would say that they were thankful

a test hadn't been as hard as they'd thought it would be or for something that had happened on the playground, or even for time they'd spent with Bill or me on the drive to school that morning. (I loved that one!) It was, I found, a sweet and revealing window into our kids' inner lives—a way to learn a little bit more about what was important to them and why.

Over time, the ritual acquired its own set of rules. One was that you couldn't repeat someone else's answer—you had to come up with your own. Another was that you couldn't judge or negate someone else's contribution. (This was helpful for me, who frequently made my three children indulge me as I went on about the sun peeking out through the gray Seattle sky or the beautiful song of a tiny wren I'd noticed while walking outside. No judgments, kids!)

Another rule was that we started dinner this way even if we had guests—and guests were always invited to contribute as well. It turned out to be a chance to get to know a side of my kids' friends that didn't always come through in other settings.

And even if the substance of a given night's set of answers didn't quite connect to gratitude in its purest form ("I'm grateful that we had a fire drill so our quiz got canceled!"), the ritual itself began to feel important. It meant that every night, regardless of what else was going on, whether we sat down that night in a happy mood or a heavy one, we spent part of that day talking to the people we loved about what mattered to us. The little dinner-time routine we adopted became, as the best rituals are, a chance to grow closer and go deeper.

~

In yoga, there's an instruction you hear frequently: "Root to rise." In a literal sense, it's a reminder to establish your center of gravity, to firmly plant your feet or your sit bones—or whatever part of your body happens to be closest to the earth—before attempting a new pose or posture.

But the metaphor works in a broader sense, too. A sapling can't know how its branches will develop and grow and bud, but it sends its roots deeper and deeper into the ground with the understanding that, whatever comes, a strong foundation will be key to its steadiness and stability. The routines and rituals and relationships that we all develop as we grow into ourselves serve as roots, keeping us grounded and secure when transitions come along to shape our branches in unpredictable ways.

I mentioned earlier that during my time at Microsoft, no matter what else was going on that day, my colleague Charlotte and I would meet around 4 to go jogging together. It might seem like a small thing, this daily bit of exercise, but the routine helped Charlotte and me blow off steam from our incredibly intense jobs, and it also formed the basis of our friendship, one of the deepest and most important relationships in my life.

Like the routine of going for a jog every day or the ritual of celebrating a birthday with cake and a card, maintaining friendships like the one Charlotte and I share can have a nourishing effect on our lives—making us healthier not just in spirit, but in body. One data point: In 2023, the US surgeon general released a report on loneliness arguing that "the mortality impact of being socially disconnected is similar to that caused by smoking up to 15 cigarettes a day."

I didn't have longevity in mind when I formed the Lunch Bunch after I left Microsoft in 1996. Honestly, I just thought it would be fun! But it ended up leading to something so much more meaningful.

In its first iteration, the Lunch Bunch was exactly what it sounds like: a group of nine women who ate lunch together once a month. Most of us either worked in the tech industry or were married to someone who did. There was no agenda for our lunches, and sometimes I'm sure we kept the conversation pretty light. Often, though, we'd talk about our families—and more specifically our kids, celebrating milestones and transitions in their lives.

A lot of us were new mothers, and someone would almost always have something to share about how her son was finally sleeping through the night or her daughter had taken her first steps. In that way, our monthly lunches became an informal opportunity to do the same thing for one another that my mother used to do through her cards: to let each other know that these things that were happening in our lives and families mattered, that they deserved our attention, that they were worth pausing over and celebrating.

Eventually, after the Lunch Bunch disbanded, a subset of us came back together, this time with the explicit goal of creating a place and space to focus on spirituality and mindfulness, an effort largely shepherded by my dear friend Killian Noe.

Killian is a brilliant author and Yale-educated pastor who cofounded the Recovery Café Network, a network of communities that support people recovering from trauma and addiction. At the time I met her, she had recently moved to Seattle from Washington, DC, and in addition to the work she was doing at Recovery Café, she was on a quest to find or form supportive community in her personal life, too.

I was initially introduced to Killian through Charlotte. Although the Lunch Bunch had ended by then, and both Charlotte and I had been gone from Microsoft for many years, she and I were still getting together regularly to exercise and talk. Over time, our jogging duo became a walking group—one that soon expanded to include my close friend Emmy Neilson.

Once Killian was on the scene, she helped us take our friendship to the next level by forming what we've referred to for years as our spiritual group, a group of women who meet regularly to learn and grow together.

Under Killian's guidance, we read Henri Nouwen, the Dutch Catholic priest who wrote about our need to connect with others. We read Thomas Keating, the Trappist priest who helped to develop the Buddhism-inflected concept of "centering prayer." We read Sandra Maitri, the artist and author who works to integrate Western psychology with Eastern spirituality. We read Mark Nepo, the poet and author who wrote *The Book of Awakening* about his transformative journey in the wake of his cancer diagnosis.

As a group, we'd explore what we read together and engage in rich discussions about what we'd learned. We'd talk about how these lessons showed up in our own lives and the changes they inspired us to make. We also used our time together to meditate and keep each other accountable for maintaining our meditation practices. Eventually, we started traveling as a group, going on silent retreats, taking an unforgettable trip to India, and once, attending a "healing ceremony" on a tiny Scottish island. (I thought that last one was going to be total BS, but boy, was I wrong! It was incredibly prayerful and moving.)

At the same time, Charlotte, Emmy, Killian, and I continued to go for our weekly walks. In fact, we're still walking together. I call these three friends my Truth Council. Every Monday, we meet up in some scenic Seattle neighborhood and talk about whatever is going on in our lives. Over the years, we've accompanied each other through many challenges and changes. Emmy's first forays into dating after her husband John's death. Killian becoming an empty nester. Charlotte's son's inspiring recovery after losing his right arm in an accident. My divorce.

But sometimes (often), we spend our walks laughing so hard and hysterically that it causes people to stop and stare. I've come to appreciate that even the parts of the walks we spend laughing serve an important spiritual purpose. The reason that we are able to be such good friends to each other through the difficult times is that we make each other a priority the rest of the time, too. We hold space for each other even when life is brimming with other asks of our time and attention—something I learned how to do from the big-hearted woman who brought my siblings and me to the card store so many times throughout my childhood, pausing her busy day to tend to the people around her, commemorating their setbacks and their joys.

In a lovely poem, the Harlem Renaissance poet Claude McKay describes what is possible when one plants deep roots "through rock and loam and clay." The tree he writes of lives "in rich imperial growth":

> *Touching the surface and the depth of things,*
> *Instinctively responsive unto both,*
> *Tasting the sweets of being and the stings,*
> *Sensing the subtle spell of changing forms,*
> *Like a strong tree against a thousand storms.*

Isn't that beautiful? Because what is life if not a "subtle spell of changing forms"? Beginnings that become endings. Endings that become new beginnings. And a prayer for stability amid the thousand storms, for roots that reach deeply enough through rock and loam and clay to keep us anchored through it all.

Chapter Seven

Emerge

Many years ago, when I was still relatively new to my career in philanthropy and struggling with a lot of self-doubt, I had an appointment on my calendar that was causing my anxiety to spiral: a meeting with an important government official about some work our foundation was doing on gender equality.

I had always admired this woman, and I really wanted the meeting to go well. It was important to me to do an effective job of representing the foundation, but there was a personal aspect to it as well: I was intimidated by her seemingly effortless confidence and competence and worried she would find me inexperienced. She had spent a lot more time on the global stage than I had, and I wanted to convince her I was someone who deserved this hour of her time.

The problem was that *I* wasn't totally convinced I was worthy of the meeting. So I drove myself and the people around me crazy as I obsessively prepared for it. I pored over briefing documents, internalized talking points, and memorized statistics. I kept trying to game out the conversation in my head. Anytime I imagined her asking me a question I couldn't answer, it would kickstart the whole process all over again. I wanted to be prepared for every possible eventuality.

While I took things to an extreme before that particular meeting, this was, more or less, how I prepared for pretty much everything back then. Every interview. Every speech. Even meetings at the foundation with people who worked for *me*.

"Melinda," my therapist once told me, "even if you wanted to know everything in the world, you can't possibly learn it all." I wasn't convinced. (Think about who I was married to at the time. He may not have known *everything*, but he sure gave that impression.) More than that, I didn't want consolation back then. I didn't want to lower my impossible standards. That felt like an easy way out—and I wanted to do things the *right* way, which, in my mind, almost always meant doing them the *hard* way.

In any case, when the day of the meeting arrived, the government official walked in—not with a three-inch-thick binder like the one I'd been lugging around with me for weeks, but with a single note card. It looked like she'd written maybe four bullet points on it, nothing more.

As it happened, she was brilliant. Warm, funny, and in complete command of every topic we discussed. What's more, she seemed to pull this off without pressuring herself to put on some performance of infallibility. A couple of times, she needed to refer to her little note card, and so she did. To think, all those hours I'd spent memorizing every statistic even tangentially related to the issues we were there to discuss, and I could have just jotted them down! And it would have been *fine*. Why had that option never occurred to me?

All these years later, I still take my work very seriously. And, yes, I still prepare intensely for meetings. But these days, I'm no longer driven by the same kind of insecurity. I finally believe that it's okay if I can't instantly summon exactly the right statistic to substantiate the point I'm making or if the limits to my knowledge reveal themselves. Now that I'm finally okay showing up as no one but myself, I no longer treat every appointment on my calendar as a referendum on whether I deserve to be there. It's a much gentler way to live.

~⌒

I wish I knew the secret to overcoming your fears, conquering self-doubt, and finding comfort in your own skin.

But over the last few years, as I approached the age of sixty, I finally realized that the "secret" may be nothing more than time. Time and experience.

Many of the friends I've walked through life with—other women my age—describe something similar, a new feeling of peace. This might be because just about no one, no matter who you are, gets anywhere near sixty unscathed. All of us have lost something precious on our journey here. A dear friend. A sister. A partner. A parent. A job we loved. A healthy working body we took for granted. None of us gets this far in life with everything intact.

The fact that we've made it here, though, is proof that we've survived our losses. And with that comes a certain measure of self-assurance that we can survive another. I think back to the story I mentioned earlier of the two waves traveling through the ocean, one big and one small. One of them is convinced that the looming shore heralds the end. The other recognizes that it's possible to experience a crash like that without losing yourself or your core.

By now, most of my friends my age have had occasion to prove their own resilience. We're all a little different now: wiser and less afraid and, maybe for those reasons alone, simply happier.

That's my theory. And although mine involves a lot less quantitative reasoning, it's consistent with a theory proposed by two economists, Andrew Oswald from England's University of Warwick and David Blanchflower from Dartmouth. These two scholars examined data on two million people from eighty countries and found that our happiness levels tend to follow a U-shaped curve. We enter adulthood with a high level of happiness, experience a dip in our 40s and 50s, then rebound. "Encouragingly," Dr. Oswald told *The New York Times*, "by the time you are 70, if you are still physically fit, then on average you are as happy and mentally healthy as a 20-year-old."

There is no question that the ability to enjoy this chapter of life is contingent on a huge amount of luck. There are so many for whom this season looks very different. People who are battling disease. People who are working around the clock as the caregiver for a family member. People who can't afford to retire. People who are lonely.

Still, I take comfort in that study of two million people and that smile-shaped happiness curve. I hope it means that most people find something new within themselves in this last third of their lives—that we can gain access to a reservoir of wisdom, of confidence, of *peace* in our "third act" that helps us see life differently.

There's a poem I discovered through Oprah by a poet who writes under the name MAIA. I keep a framed version on my desk and look at it just about every day.

i hope

when you come home to yourself

there are flowers lining the front porch

that were left from all the women

you were before

I think about the message of that poem in two ways. First, I read it as a reminder that, wherever we are in life, we should find a way to look back at the versions of ourselves who came before us not with shame or regret but with tenderness and compassion. The people we used to be deserve for us to remember that they knew so much less, had experienced so much less, and were doing the best they could with what they had.

That's how I'm able to look back on the version of myself who walked into that meeting I was so nervous about and feel not just unembarrassed but actually a little proud of myself for trying *so* hard, for recognizing that my role at the foundation was an amazing opportunity in life and wanting to rise to the occasion, and for summoning all the courage it took to get through the situations that used to cause me such searing anxiety.

The poem has another meaning for me, too. It also invites us to consider who we are now through the eyes of our younger selves. In that regard, it's not hard for me to imagine the woman I was back then lovingly delivering flowers to my porch to celebrate that I'm finally as con-

fident and as comfortable in my own skin as she wished
she could be.

⁓

When I turned sixty last summer, I was doing a lot of
thinking about the seasons that make up a woman's life.
Often, when I'm playing with something in my mind,
I find myself wanting to talk to other women about it.
That's how I got the idea to reach out to a few friends
and some women I've connected with through my work—
women of all different ages—to join me for a series of
conversations about the experiences that have made them
who they are.

Altogether, I spoke to seven incredible women: soccer
champion Megan Rapinoe, actress and producer Reese
Witherspoon, filmmaker and screenwriter Ava DuVernay, former First Lady Michelle Obama, broadcast icons
Oprah Winfrey and Gayle King, and tennis legend Billie
Jean King. I asked each of them about the transitions that
have defined them and received a wide range of answers.
Becoming a working mother. Navigating a major career
pivot. Coming out as a lesbian. Leaving the White House.
Surviving a spouse's betrayal. And, in Billie Jean King's
case, becoming a feminist icon after beating the pants
off the former number-one-ranked tennis player Bobby
Riggs in the famous 1973 tennis match known as the

Battle of the Sexes. (I still remember watching it at home on TV as a kid.)

I also found it moving to hear these women talk about the same aspects of life from the vantage points of different decades. Reese Witherspoon, for example, still has her youngest child at home and described the constant "ticker tape" running through her brain of what her children are up to and what they need from her. Michelle Obama, on the other hand, spoke from the perspective of a woman whose children are now grown and out of the house— still a central part of her life but no longer reliant on her to get through the day. Megan Rapinoe is one year into her retirement from professional sports, at the very beginning of her next chapter, while Billie Jean King retired forty-one years ago and has written much of that chapter already.

When I spoke to Oprah and Gayle, friends for forty-eight years, about what they've learned about themselves and each other along the way, both of them talked about developing the capacity to navigate change, the omnipresent force in all our lives. Oprah quoted the poem by MAIA and shared her own conviction that "change is there to evolve you." Gayle said something beautiful, too: "Aging is just another word for living."

I am so grateful to all these women for being candid and thoughtful about their journeys. They are such well-known and formidable figures in our culture that it felt special to get this glimpse of their internal lives—the struggles and triumphs and doubts and wisdom that have paved their paths to where they are today. After we finished our conversations and hugged goodbye, I could imagine each one of them, like the woman in the poem, coming home to herself, finding a porch lined with flowers from all the women she was before.

⁓

A few years ago, abandoning my old habit of creating a lengthy list of New Year's resolutions, I started choosing a single "word of the year" to encapsulate my aspirations for the twelve months ahead. One year, I chose *gentle*, a reminder to go easy on myself and fight the pull of perfectionism. Another, I chose *spacious* and spent the year encouraging myself to make room for the things that matter.

Some years, it can be hard to settle on a word. And some years, the word announces itself with great clarity. That was the case as I sat down in late 2023 to pick a word for 2024. There was only one choice, and it was obvious: 2024, the year I started writing this book, has been my year of *transition*.

During this season, I've seen my life change in ways I hoped for, ways I fought against, and ways I never could have imagined. At fifty-eight, much earlier in life than I expected, I became a grandmother. After nearly two decades of having children at home, I am now an empty nester. After nearly three decades with a man I loved, our marriage is over, and I have moved on. After baking my values into a foundation that I thought would be the center of my life's work, I am beginning a new chapter in my philanthropy more specifically focused on women and families. Already, I'm working with new partners, trying new philanthropic approaches, and deploying significant resources to help level the playing field for women and girls.

As I enter this new chapter in my life and work, I am keeping in mind the lesson I've learned over and over again: What matters most is not what happens *to* us but *how we respond* to those events, both in the moment and, really quite importantly, on the next day. Because what we do on that next day is what makes us who we are and how we make our lives our own. This is true in all kinds of transitions, happy or sad, welcome or unwanted.

A few years ago, my friend Killian introduced me to the work of the late Irish poet John O'Donohue. I've been thinking lately of a poem of his called "For a New Beginning." It opens like this:

> *In the out-of-the-way places of the heart,*
> *Where your thoughts never think to wander,*
> *This beginning has been quietly forming,*
> *Waiting until you were ready to emerge.*

I began writing this book while I was in the middle of this season of transition. I am finishing it in the same place. I don't have a tidy conclusion to draw from the experience yet. I still haven't reached the other side. But this journey has renewed my faith that even on our darkest, most difficult days, somewhere deep within us, a new beginning is quietly forming. That has been true for me, and whatever it is that you are going through right now, I hope it's true for you, too.

You may not be able to see it yet, name it yet, or know it yet. But that flicker of anticipation, that promise of a new beginning, is what helps us keep moving forward—empowering us to emerge from all we have lived through still fully alive and available to the possibilities that await us on the next day.

Acknowledgments

There are so many people I want to thank for their role in this book and the journey that led me to write it.

To Charlotte, Emmy, Killian, and Mary—four of the most important people in my life—thank you for our deep and enduring friendship. As these pages attest, in good times and bad, you are the people I want to be near. Thank you also to my spiritual groups—the SWADs and Zero Circle—for keeping me on the path to spiritual growth and for all the ways that our time together has enriched my life.

At the Gates Foundation, the center of my work for almost twenty-five years, I want to thank the entire staff, past and present: You are truly a world-class team. In particular, thank you to Mark Suzman for his steady leadership during a period of enormous transition and to the board for their wise and effective guidance. I'm also infinitely grateful to the foundation's partners—people and organizations working on the front lines of some of the world's most intractable challenges. Through your optimism that progress is possible and your compassion for the people whose lives your work touches, you are writing the story of a better world.

A long list of people contributed to this book. First, I am immensely grateful to Clare Krupin. For more than a decade, Clare has been a profoundly thoughtful writing partner as we have traveled the world together, capturing stories of the people we met. You wouldn't be reading this book if she hadn't been alongside me on this journey, asking the questions that helped me reflect on exactly what I wanted to write and encouraging me at every turn.

I'm also grateful to Kate Hanske, Elizabeth Heu, Emily Jones, and Meg Tuomala for their research; Julie Tate for her thoughtful, thorough approach to helping me get the facts right; and Anu Arora for her deep reservoir of wisdom, teachings, and poetry. A very special thank-you to Andy Barr, whose talent, experience, and insight made this book better. (He also lived up to his reputation for being extremely funny.)

At Flatiron, I want to thank Megan Lynch as well as Marlena Bittner, Malati Chavali, Kukuwa Fraser, Keith Hayes, Kate Keating, Cat Kenney, and Katherine Turro. To Will Schwalbe, one of the world's greatest editors, thank you for helping me give the words on the page a beating heart. Six years ago, when we started our collaboration on *The Moment of Lift*, you wisely counseled me that the stories that made me feel most vulnerable to share were precisely the ones to keep, not cut, because it is in those shadowed places of ourselves that we are most able to connect with others. You didn't have to remind me of that as many times with this book—but only because I now hear your voice in my head, encouraging me along. Thank you.

I am indebted to my whole team at Pivotal for the deep care and expertise you bring to the important work you do to improve the lives of women and families and replace barriers with possibilities. Special thanks to Haven Ley, Josh Lozman, Erin Harkless Moore, Hallie Ross, Paul Silva, and Renee Wittemyer for sharing your perspectives on my first draft and helping me improve it—and to Alex Morgan and Amy Rainey for helping bring this project to life. And, as always, thank you to Benjamin Caryl, Amy Johnston, Jediah Jones, Abby Page, and Shane Smith for helping me carve out space and time for my priorities both at work and at home.

Also at Pivotal, I want to thank Courtney Wade, Brooke Anderson, and John Sage—three people whose job titles come nowhere near describing the indispensable role they play in my life and work. Courtney, for almost ten years I've relied on your strategic vision, your creativity, and your frequent thought partnership. I'm grateful to you for helping me use my voice to more effectively advocate for women and girls and advance the issues that matter most in their lives. Brooke, thank you for your superhuman ability to look around corners, your visionary leadership of this organization, and your deep commitment to making sure our impact is seen and felt in people's lives. You have spent your career working on big, audacious goals at the highest levels, and we are so lucky to have your experience and perspective elevating all we do. John, over the course of our long partnership, you've changed jobs no less than six times to help get me where I am. You are both a truth teller and one of my most trusted confidants, and I am so glad that John Neilson convinced you not to move to Kuala Lumpur because I can't imagine my life or career without you.

This book also benefited enormously from candid personal conversations I had with Ava DuVernay, Billie Jean King, Gayle King, Michelle Obama, Megan Rapinoe, Oprah Winfrey, and Reese Witherspoon—all of whom have broken barriers for women in such notable ways. As a mother and a grandmother, I am so grateful that role models like you exist. (I still remember what Billie Jean's example meant to me as a young girl!) Count me as yet another woman who has been moved and inspired by all you do.

I would additionally like to thank the counselors and

the therapists, the poets and the writers, and the spiritual teachers from all walks of life for devoting yourselves to such noble professions. Thank you for lending your training, your thinking, your gifts, and your guidance to the people around you—and for being there for people like me when we need you most. Keep doing your beautiful, critically necessary work.

There's another person I want to thank. You've helped me heal and find beauty again. You know who you are.

Finally, my family—the greatest blessing of my life. Mom and Dad, I hope it gives you tremendous pride to know that the values you embedded in the four of us early and often continue to shape our lives, our children's lives, and now *their* children's lives. That is the most important gift you could have given us, and it has made all the difference.

To my siblings—Susan, Raymond, and Steven—thank you for being there in hard times and joyous ones and for the humor you've infused into our family life, making it impossible for any of us to ever take ourselves too seriously.

Most of all, my love and gratitude to Phoebe, Rory, Jenn, and Nayel. No mother (or mother-in-law) has ever been prouder. I have watched all four of you launch your own unique journeys to advocate for the things you care about in your own unique ways. You absolutely live your values and use those values to guide your work. I have learned so much from all four of you and love each one of you for exactly who you are.

Leila and Mia, I could not be more excited to be your Nonna. Now that you are on this planet, my commitment to unlocking a better future for women and girls everywhere has only grown stronger. I love you.

Credits

About the Author

Melinda French Gates is a philanthropist, businesswoman, and global advocate for women and girls. For more than twenty-five years, Melinda has led efforts to unlock a healthier, more prosperous, more equal future. Today, she heads Pivotal, an organization she formed in 2015 that works to accelerate the pace of progress and advance women's power and influence in the United States and around the world. Previously, she founded and cochaired the Gates Foundation, where, for more than two decades, she set the direction and priorities of the world's largest philanthropy. Melinda is also the author of the bestselling book *The Moment of Lift* and the creator of Moment of Lift Books, an imprint publishing original nonfiction by visionaries working to unlock a more equal world.

Melinda grew up in Dallas, Texas, and attended Duke University, where she received a bachelor's degree in computer science and economics and an MBA. She spent the first decade of her career developing multimedia products at Microsoft before leaving the company to focus on her family and philanthropic work. Melinda has three children—Jenn, Rory, and Phoebe—and lives in Seattle, Washington.